THE CITY AT THREE P.M.

THE CITY AT THREE P.M.

WRITING, READING, AND TRAVELING

Peter LaSalle

DZANC
BOOKS

5220 Dexter Ann Arbor Rd.
Ann Arbor, MI 48103
www.dzancbooks.org

The essays in this collection originally appeared (sometimes in different form and under different titles) in: *Agni* ("Metaphysical Messages: With J.L.B. in Buenos Aires" and "Walking: Another Essay on Writing"); *Another Chicago Magazine* ("Plasticize Your Documents: With G. Flaubert in Tunisia); *Creative Nonfiction* ("The City at Three P.M.: An Essay on Writing"); *The Literary Review* ("What Plays in France: Observations on American Writing Anointed in the Republic"); *Memoir Journal* ("Two Short Movies and a Transcendent Trailer: With N. West in Hollywood"); *The Nation* ("Jamaica, 1976: How Far the Poet's Writ Runs"); *Profils Américains*, France ("The Saul Bellow Speeding Ticket"); *The Providence Sunday Journal* ("Ireland, 1971: About Christy Brown"); *Tin House* ("The Other Life of Any Book: Three Copies of Malcolm Lowry's *Under the Volcano*"); and *Worldview* (Cameroon, 1979: Buma Kor & Co.). "Walking: Another Essay on Writing" also appeared in *The Best American Travel Writing 2010* (Houghton Mifflin), edited by Bill Buford and Jason Wilson; "Two Short Movies and a Transcendent Trailer: With N. West in Hollywood" received the 2012 Editors' Prize from *Memoir Journal*.

The author is grateful to the editors of these publications and also for the support of the Susan Taylor McDaniel Regents Professorship in Creative Writing at the University of Texas at Austin.

Designed by Steven Seighman

Library of Congress Cataloging-in-Publication Data
LaSalle, Peter.
    The city at three p.m. : writing, reading, and traveling / by Peter LaSalle.
    pages cm
    ISBN 978-1-938103-20-9 1. Literary landmarks. 2. Travel writing. 3. Books and reading. I. Title.
    PN164.L27 2015 809—dc23   2015008019

First U.S. Edition: December 2015

Printed in the United States of America

10 9 8 7 6 5 4 3 2 1

For three good friends—Alex MacLean, Don Graham, and, in memory, Ivan Teixeira

CONTENTS

I have journeyed in quest of a book.

—Borges, "The Library of Babel"

THE SAUL BELLOW SPEEDING TICKET

Saul Bellow crazy, I drove the Interstate from Rhode Island out to Chicago in the fall of 1971 in a sputtering blue Plymouth Duster. The junk packed enough pep, however, to attract the attention of a radar-wielding state trooper somewhere in the farmland flatness of western New York right before you hit Erie. As he scrawled out a speeding ticket, he seemed as surprised as I was that I'd gotten the thing up to the ninety-one miles an hour at which he had clocked me.

I always thought the incident was somehow in the spirit of those Saul Bellow sentences that had done such a number on me at the time in *Mr. Sammler's Planet* or *Augie March*—reckless and a little out of control, but solid in their genuine direction, nevertheless, which was what made them so pure.

I was in a hurry. I was enrolling to take a master's in English, with a creative writing concentration, at the University of Chicago for the simple reason that Bellow was there.

It didn't take me long to learn (I still can't believe I hadn't read the fat graduate school catalog more carefully on this) that Bellow himself wasn't even a member of the English department at the university's gray gothic campus on the city's South Side, with the glassy new Regenstein Library—built smack on the spot where Fermi and company had first achieved nuclear fission in a makeshift underground lab—adding at least a touch of modernism to the otherwise prevailing staid architecture. Dick Stern was the resident novelist in the English department, and he explained to a very disappointed me that Bellow—who taught literature and philosophy, it seemed, rather than any creative writing—was a member of the faculty of the Committee on Social Thought. Said "committee" turned out to be a decidedly elite degree program for carefully selected advanced Ph.D. students, interdisciplinary and maybe the kind of pedagogically nonconformist operation that could exist only at a place like U. of Chicago, which in its utter intellectualism then—and probably now—had to be the closest thing to a real European university here in America. (Once a Big Ten sports school with the famous coach Amos Alonzo Stagg at the gridiron helm, Chicago eventually relegated football to the status of a mere club; it was almost an ongoing parody of intercollegiate athletics when I was there, supposedly a varsity sport again but in essence remaining more of a club, as the bunch of nerdy guys who sometimes had trouble buckling the football helmet chin straps under their beards played their games to marching-band music supplied by assorted fellow undergrads in street clothes happily blowing away on kazoos. Honestly.)

Stern was a big, kind, energetic specimen, and he told me there was no reason to feel let down—in his big and kind and entirely energetic way, he assured me that Bellow was a "great guy." He said he would do some of the spadework for me, mention my name, and all I had to do after that was to drop by during Bellow's office hours to see The Man himself.

Which I often did.

The first time, Bellow was at his administrative desk, his post as chairman of the Committee on Social Thought. As the secretary ushered me in, what struck me, besides the impeccable haberdashery of a double-breasted, dark blue wool blazer and maroon silk foulard tie, was the pile of paperwork he was plowing through. It looked like forms to be filled out, paper-clipped-together dissertation proposals too, maybe, and I was amazed that this eminence who hadn't quite won the Nobel Prize yet, though he had won nearly everything else on the literary front in this country and much abroad, was occupying himself with such mundane matters. On other occasions I sat across a big desk from him in his personal office upstairs in that same building with its standard U. of C. gargoyles under the eaves, usually the only student coming to see him. My good luck on that count surprised me. While I didn't take particular note each visit of what he was wearing, it seems to stick in my mind that the outfit was often a well-tailored silvery suit more fit for a high-rolling international businessman than an academic, or possibly it was just the way that the silver light poured through the mullioned windows behind him and his hair itself being very silver that rendered him, well, such a presence (vision?). The steam heat radiators clanked, occasionally somebody thundered up or down the stairwell in the corridor, and soon I realized that Stern had been right, Bellow was a great guy, willing to listen to my own talk about reading, also my talk about work and travels since finishing college, all of which I blabbed and blabbed to him.

I once asked him why, to be frank, with all the money he had obviously made on his books, had he returned to teach at a university, anyway; to which he replied, somewhat softly, "Where else could I go?" I felt an idiot for even asking it, the answer was so simple and so damn right. I remember my going on during another visit about how I'd hastily fled a city newspaper job and lived in Dublin the year before. There I worked on my own writing and did some freelance journalism, even hooked up for a while with the fine, and quite raucous, Irish writer Christy Brown, who was handicapped due to cerebral palsy and typed with his toes. I had interviewed him for a feature article and then sometimes helped him with tasks like answering fan mail from the load of it that flooded in from the U.S. after the success of his bestselling autobiographical novel about growing up in a rough Dublin slum, *Down All the Days*, later largely the basis of the award-winning movie *My Left Foot*. Bellow wanted to hear all the details, from a description of Christy's flat in Dublin's city-owned housing (the little living room's red linoleum, the cheesy hi-fi, the cadre of working-class Brown brothers who spent less time working now that Christy, suddenly well-off, had made it and who hung around that Kimmage flat in frilly Mod suits)—yes, everything from specifics of the premises to a play-by-play description of how ever-smiling Christy managed to actually pick up a sheet of yellow foolscap with his left foot and put it into the Smith-Corona electric placed on the floor, to start writing another story or poem. In grad school I was avidly immersed in John Hawkes's edgy, surreal fare, and one day I told Bellow of my enthusiasm. Bellow himself didn't exactly appreciate Hawkes's novels, and there in the office something seemed to have clicked for him.

"Hawkes," Bellow said, smiling with his gapped front teeth and his head perking, as apparently a thought just came to mind.

"What?" I said.

"Hawkes," he continued, "this is it—if your friend Christy Brown in Ireland types with his toes, maybe Hawkes types with his arse!"

Perfect.

The year wound down. I did manage to earn an M.A. in my several months of residence, Stern helping me with his overseeing some independent study courses for credit and my using for a thesis a novel I had written in Ireland about the usual Catholic-boyhood hijinks. Bellow was generous enough to read the entire novel, stressing I was a writer, as far as he was concerned, but gingerly suggesting that in this attempt I was working a vein that Joyce and James T. Farrell had pretty much thoroughly mined years before. By way of Stern, the manuscript was returned to me with a note from Bellow saying as much. I knew by then the novel wasn't very substantial, and I thought I was already writing better stuff, so it wasn't a crushing assessment. I ran into Bellow crossing the campus quadrangles, and he invited me to stroll with him for a bit to discuss what he had said in the note. It was one of those almost warm spring afternoons in Chicago where the grass is green and the fleshy crocuses are starting to puff from their loam beds, but you'd still best wear heavy clothes if you have any sense about you, Bellow that day in a black homburg and spiffy topcoat. More so than Bellow's explanation of his critique of my novel, what probably interested me at that stage, sad to say, was being *seen* with Bellow by other students, the two of us walking together and chatting like that (there was a certain M.A. student—a pretty girl with gray eyes and strawberry-blond hair named Harriet who had a part-time job as an editorial researcher in the downtown offices of *Playboy*, no less—and I was at long last making progress toward a dating relationship with her), but I do remember one comment from Bellow then, his saying, "Character is everything, Peter," and he liked my sense of character in the manuscript. I suppose I can say now that the most magnetic thing about Bellow was that like any of his own fictional protagonists— Herzog or Henderson or the wonderful Augie himself—he wielded a real fullness of personality: part wisecracker, part clotheshorse, part Big-Hearted Otis, and a giant part keen intellectual. He was a character and he was indeed a great guy, as Stern would have it, and in all my subsequent years of teaching I have learned that such is the one rare ingredient that surely makes for a special teacher, or special writer, when you think of it—that quality as simple as being a "great guy," male or female.

People I ran into later who knew Bellow well would ask me if he was even approachable then, because they remembered that my particular year of study was the time when he was apparently having little luck in his final drive to assemble what turned out to be for me his masterpiece, *Humboldt's Gift*. They claimed he was cranky during that.

Not a chance, I told them.

✄

And again, could there be any moment finer in life for a young, would-be writer than to be so excited that you let your desert boot get the better of your judgment on the accelerator, as you glanced in the rearview mirror to notice a red roof beacon pulsatingly flashing? And about to be clipped for fifty bucks or so in fines that you really couldn't afford to shell out at a time when you were close to flat broke, at least you had been speeding for a noble cause, maybe not just toward the City of Chicago and Saul Bellow reportedly there, but now—with the drudgery of a stretch of newspaper work well behind you and a novel manuscript packed lovingly in your own battered suitcase (only later would you admit it was apprentice work, imitative)—you were racing as fast as that body-rotted Duster could carry you toward what you saw awaiting in the distance as the nicest of all ideas—a future with a life where Literature itself, with the old capital *L*, would hopefully always matter.

But for the moment there *was* the cop car behind me, my stomach already no more than a nest of slithering grass snakes. I pulled over to the breakdown lane.

I would have to learn to take my time.

1998, FROM *PROFILS AMÉRICAINS* (FRANCE)

METAPHYSICAL MESSAGES: WITH J.L.B. IN BUENOS AIRES

1. Where I Am

I'm in downtown Buenos Aires, alone, and I'm heading toward Calle Tucumán. It's the end of the Argentine summer, the first week in March, 2002.

2. The Mirror that Remains

Buenos Aires is hot, but often as handsome as everybody always told you it is. There are wide, straight boulevards thick with cafés and impressive pseudo-French wedding-cake architecture, plenty of plane trees and feathery jacarandas, flower gardens still blooming. There are also a lot of crumbling newer low high-rises. And there is soot from noisy taxis and buses tangible in the humid air, old window air conditioners above you hosingly dripping onto the crowded sidewalks. Said sidewalks can be outright hazardous with broken tiles, and every few blocks there is maybe yet another woman in ragged Indian dress sitting on that sidewalk with a baby or two and holding up a plastic cup, begging, as the rather chic Porteño downtown population, noticeably Euro-looking, goes this way and that in the coming twilight. Which is to say, the city also appears complicated, even a little seedy sometimes.

I've traveled to Buenos Aires to spend a couple of weeks for no other reason than I want to see if I can tune in on a bit of Borges's metaphysic—meaning the metaphysical insight and airy transport—in the place where it all happened. In the morning I sit around my hotel. First a spot called Hotel Central Córdoba on Calle San Martín, across from the fa-mous jewelry shop that regularly supplied Evita's spangles, I learn, then moving to a better spot up the street called Hotel Phoenix, where Edward Prince of Wales once stayed when the Phoenix had been legitimately swank and where they give me an oversize corner room on the top floor of the turn-of-the-century place with three balustraded balconies; the center one offers a view right down Avenida Córdoba to the docks and a fine slice of the cinnamon river, the muddy Plata. I read Borges in the morning, either the New Directions copy of *Labyrinths* I brought or the stack of his poems I photostatted back in Austin, yes, I reread the work I've read probably a dozen times before, always discovering something new to me. Then in the afternoon I head out to some of the places important in his biography, also a nice way to get to know such a large city. This is a different kind of a trip for me, not running around to line up interviews with writers or do library research on a country's literature, as I have done—admittedly happily so—in places like Ire-land and Central Africa and India, occasionally with some lecturing, too; now it is just me with Borges's writing, in the city that was so dear to him, that defined him to the outside world as much as he also defined it to the outside world. I have gone into the entire thing with little direction other than that, to be honest, and sometimes the project seems foolish, to be five thousand or so miles away from my home base with no practical, concrete game plan. But sometimes it more than works out, as it will today.

A government tourism office has told me about the Museo Solar Natal Jorge Luis Borges on Tucumán. Tucumán is one of the main cross streets above the Plaza de Mayo; that's the park you always see in the news clips where the massive demonstrations go on in front of the very pink Casa Rosada, the presidential palace. (The fascistic rallies for the Peróns transpired there; the Mothers of the Plaza de Mayo, never letting Argentines forget the literally thousands killed during the reign of the vicious military officers in the 1970s-80s, themselves still march there every Thursday afternoon at three.) I stop before a white two-story building at number 840 Tucumán here in the downtown, a vaguely Neoclassical masonry structure with some frilly trim. There is a plaque on it saying B. was indeed born on the premises in 1899, back then the home of Borges's maternal grandparents; the birthplace, or *solar natal*, is now a YWCA. Sandwiched between it and another old building is a newer storefront setup, one-story, almost what you might find at a strip mall in the States. The big blue plastic lettering on the corrugated gray metal atop the glass front says "MUSEO JORGE LUIS BORGES," though an overhead steel grating is pulled to the sidewalk and padlocked there. With my hands cupped I look inside, to see the place is empty, just deep-yellow walls and a royal-blue floor, poster-paint hues, and nothing else within;

whatever displays of manuscripts and photographs and mementos, etc., there once were here are completely gone. I go into the YWCA, its open marble lobby. Continuing through a set of inside doors and past a bronze bust of Borges, I find a rear patio and a small office with a counter. A white-haired woman standing up and shuffling through some papers on a desk doesn't notice me at first, and when she does, she gives me the kind of suspicious squint that I guess is universal when such a party confronts any middle-aged male poking around a YWCA.

In Spanish, I ask her about the museum, but she tells me it is closed down. I ask her for how long, and she says since last December, which means that it might have folded right around the time that the entire Argentine economy crashed like the Hindenburg on a particularly bad day; she advises I head up to the Centro Cultural Borges. I've already seen the small display they have on his life in that too culturally conscious new arts complex, named after him but principally devoted to dance recitals and art exhibitions and foreign films. Nevertheless, possibly still feeling a little creepy myself for poking around a YWCA, I energetically thank the woman for the valuable tip, which seems to be what she wants to hear.

Outside, I look back into the closed museum. That one front room deserted, then a door opening to a smaller back room, just as empty. And I confirm what I *thought* I saw. There is, in fact, one item left—a single large, round, unframed mirror on the back yellow wall, which reflects me smack in the middle of it as portrayed looking into it, through the grating and glass with cupped hands. I take out my little pocket notebook and Bic. I write down that it is *more than ironic* that Borges confessed throughout his life that he had always harbored a terror of mirrors, the watery way they attest to our own incorporeality and even ghostliness, or constantly double us to the point we are not sure if we are *who* we really are, and now in a museum devoted to documenting his life (the museum was created in 1999, a brochure I have tells me, by the Asociación Borgesiana de Buenos Aires) the only thing that remains, triumphant in a way, is a single mirror.

I get a woozy rush of the metaphysic I came in search of, if you want to know the truth, and the purpose of the trip doesn't seem mere whimsy at all right then.

3. Maps

The map of the city I've gotten from a tourism office is laid out so what is north is on the lower half, what is south at the top. You read it that way. I get a different map from a different tourism office (but like the other map, with ads for local bars and boutiques, on glossy full-colored paper), and it also has the same upside-down configuration.

4. The Hooker, Decidedly High Class

It's a couple of days later, night now.

I've bought some books in Buenos Aires bookstores that have given me solid information on Borges and the city. Several local proper scholars have already done professionally, and much better, what I'm doing as an amateur, tracking down not only the biographically important sites but also many places alluded to in the stories and poems, even the essays. And, of course, Borges's essays are not to be forgotten, and included in that New Directions *Labyrinths*, a volume that blends many of the stories from the seminal 1944 book

Ficciones (which some say changed the look of world fiction forever) with a scattering of nonfiction pieces, is the flatly amazing (mind-blowing?) two-part piece, "A New Refutation of Time." For me it's a powerful treatise on the outright fluidity of what we sometimes believe, mistakenly, clocks are rather rigidly trying to tell us, commentary akin to that in Eliot's *Four Quartets,* but with a more direct daring in the leaps of thought, less hemming and hawing about it; I've already reread that essay twice while in Buenos Aires.

No guidebook is needed to find the address where Borges lived the largest chunk of his adult life, between 1944 and 1985, most of that period as a bachelor with his mother. That is my specific mission this evening—to take a good look at the spot that I have already passed a dozen times or more in my wandering around. Actually, it's tough to miss the place. The very image of an older, cloudy-eyed Borges, who was for a long while often ignored at home during his lifetime, now has become as much of an icon in Argentina as a smiling blond Evita or the wider-smiling, slickly-coiffed legendary tango crooner Carlos Gardel, and as you come out of the subway at the San Martín stop, there at the top of the posh pedestrian walkway for upscale shopping, Calle Florida, a lit plastic sign with a map gives the principal attractions of the Plaza San Martín/Retiro district, including an orange bull's-eye dot for item "H" on the plan: Casa de Borges. It's only a few streets over from both hotels where I have been staying, in fact.

Nine-ninety-four Calle Maipú is an eight-story apartment building of functional gray concrete architecture, maybe from the 1930s, built on the corner of narrow Maipú and equally narrow Charcas, also called Calle M. T. de Alvear.

Borges's place was on the seventh floor, and stepping back, looking up from across the street, I can see the apartment, recessed and right under another on the very top floor; it has a terrace with a sort of ship's pipe railing, green awnings shading the windows, and a line of potted plants on the terrace itself. It is said that Borges's own bedroom was just a tiny one, with a stubby cot, a night table, and a bookcase. His widowed mother had the apartment's larger master bedroom, which he kept as almost a shrine to her after she died; reportedly, he announced even then when he came into the apartment at night, "Mother, I'm home." He also had a white cat, Beppo, shown in some photos rolling around the carpet on its back and boxing maybe imaginary butterflies. The neighborhood is a good one, near Calle Florida and across from the quite formal, more-than-leafy Plaza San Martín, a British-style park, and just around the corner from a shop stocked with a large supply of high-priced polo gear. Next to the apartment building's lobby is a women's clothing boutique, where the ground-floor exterior has been given a reddish polished-stone overlay. While I take more notes, looking through the glass doors to that small white-marble lobby with its elevator and twin Art Nouveau marble staircases, cramped and curving, a group of attractive, hiply dressed young women come out of the boutique; they are closing up for the night, locking the pulled-down galvanized shutter and talking. I keep taking notes, writing by the streetlight, nobody else but the young women around. I like the idea that Borges wrote much of his major work here, my being at the spot, and I move backward a step or two as one of the young women from the shop walks by in front of me. I keep taking notes on the layout of the place, the way it faces the corner, with a separate plane of the building there to make for a façade of three sides; across Charcas is an edifice in full-fledged Louvre style, an officers' club and a military museum. A half dozen of what can sometimes seem like the millions of black-and-yellow Buenos Aires taxis now stop for the light at the intersection, then move on. Borges commented in later life about the growing problem of this intersection's traffic noise, which must get bad during the day. In a poem from the stack of them I photostatted to bring with me, "The Leaves of the Cypress" (actually a prose poem), he offers a wonderfully haunting little account of a dream in which Death comes up to his apartment right here on Maipú and takes him for what seems a test ride to the cemetery: "At the corner of Charcas and Maipú, outside the tenement, a carriage was waiting. With a formal gesture tantamount to an order, he directed me to step in first."

I glance up to see that the young woman is walking by me again. She is tall, a long-haired brunette with high cheekbones, wearing trim beige slacks, strapped heels, and a knit black top; she smiles at me and I nod. She looks classy, perhaps "Upper East Sidish," and it's only when I move on and notice her now walking back and forth in front of a hotel down Charcas a ways, a doorman and another guy standing beside him smilingly ogling her as she passes, do I realize that she wasn't with the others closing up the store at all. She is a hooker, and what I come to learn in subsequent trips to scout out the area is that this whole pocket is a favorite one for very classy hookers. Some stroll the streets alone, groups of them chat and laugh outside of normal-looking bar/lounges that are actually a part of the business, like one called "Friday's Club" (*not* a TGIF franchise), which faces the closed-down old Harrods department store. In Argentina prostitution has been legal since the Perón regime.

The next morning, thinking about the encounter, I suppose I feel naïve for not spotting her as a hooker right off. Some man of the world I am—I mean, there I was lost in what most of my life has been lost in, these obsessive imaginings in and about literature, wildly taking notes, and I didn't even know enough about how the real world works to recognize a hooker when I saw one, when I was *solicited* by one. It leads me to rereading another Borges poem I have photostatted for the trip, "Remorse," where Borges says he never fulfilled the basic message of life that his kind, caring parents wished to instill in him—simply to be happy. "I wasn't happy. My ways/ Have not fulfilled their youthful hope. I gave/ My mind to the symmetric stubbornness/ Of art, and all its web of pettiness."

I hope it's not going to turn out to be one of those brooding trips where, given the solitary, idle time that travel alone affords, you start evaluating every little thing, which often echoes every big thing, in your life. (The women you didn't marry over the years, the way that lately you haven't seen enough of, and seem to have drifted away from, your own immediate family all living elsewhere, which would break your own dead parents' hearts—that variety of dangerous thinking.) If I hit the metaphysic at the closed-down museum with the mirror, I know I came up completely empty in that department with my do-si-doing with the young woman, the smiling hooker, there in front of the Casa de Borges the previous balmy night, big yellow clouds floating by the half-full moon.

5. Other Spots

I keep reading at the hotel in the morning (the Phoenix, where I eventually settle after a hydrofoil-ferry ride across the wide Plata and a few days in a small coastal town in Uruguay, which seems to be a sweet, sweet country), then walking more in the afternoon, right into the evening. I sometimes use city buses, the subway, too; I check out more Borges landmarks. A bunch of single Australian women book into the otherwise quite empty hotel for a weeklong conference for tango aficionados, and they are fun to talk to at breakfast in the hotel dining room. They speak enthusiastically about tango as if it is a way of life, a yoga. Among them is a physical therapist from Sydney named Brendie, not far from my own age and with a strikingly good figure, probably from all that hearty tangoing (she knows it, likes wearing low-cut leotard tops); she has large dark eyes fringed with incipient crow's feet, a toothy smile, and what we used to call a Prince Valiant haircut, black. Quieter than the others, she does invite me to go to a professional tango concert offered as part of the conference one evening, though I duck out, telling myself that, if nothing else, innocently flirting with a woman like Brendie at breakfast is really more like my usual territory, and I've never been a hooker kind of guy. So how should I have been *expected* to know what was going on in front of the Casa de Borges?

Buenos Aires in March sometimes seems absurdly hot, ninety degrees and ninety percent humidity. It's tough even on me, somebody who has lived in central Texas for more than twenty years and should be accustomed to anything a summer can dish out. The end-of-the-day thunderstorms— brief but inundating, the gusts bending the tall palm trees in the parks—don't manage to usher in any relief and just make the humidity worse. I go out to the Palermo neighborhood of Borges's childhood, originally a barrio of diverse immigrants and where the established and relatively well-to-do Borges family (his ancestry shows many Argentine notables, including nineteenth-century military commanders on both sides) moved when Borges was very young. It was in Palermo that Borges immersed himself in his father's extensive English library, and I never fail to get a kick out of the detail of how bilingual Borges first read *Don Quixote* as a child in an English translation, which was right before the father, a lawyer, took the family to live in Europe for several years. Palermo looks yuppified now; the Borges had a substantial two-story home on Calle Serrano (today Calle Jorge Luis Borges, where the original house is gone), though the neighborhood back then was apparently still a little rough, with tango barrooms and the kind of knife-fighting characters found in B.'s many realistic, and often overlooked, short stories about Buenos Aires street life. Nearby I find other homes the family lived in. There's no grave to visit; Borges died in Switzerland in 1986 only weeks after marrying his former student and companion/secretary María Kodama— she was thirty-nine, he almost eighty-seven—and is buried in Geneva.

I ride on a rattling red bus with goofy whitewall tires (the breeze through the windows is nice) to ramshackle La Boca, farther south and toward the mouth of the river, where the tango was reportedly born. In La Boca, touristy tango nightspots still thrive in the makeshift old buildings with their distinctive corrugated metal sides painted wildly bright colors. One Sunday morning, walking the length of the long

park that runs next to a wildlife refuge on the river, an esplanade called the Costanera Sur not far from downtown,
I seem to recognize the asterisk-shaped cast-iron patterning repeatedly inset in the old, formal cement railings of the
walkway. I wonder where I have seen that. Then I remember. There is a great picture in nearly all the books about
Borges's life—not only my on-the-scene guidebooks but also
the standard biographies I read before the trip—and it shows
a dark-haired younger Borges in a good suit standing beside
a petite, pretty young woman in a summer dress who is sitting on that railing, Estela Canto, in March 1945; Borges
was head-over-heels for her, but the relationship didn't work
out. In the photo, Estela, long curly hair and daintily snub-
nosed, has a white purse and open-toed white shoes, and she
is holding up for the camera a copy of a book on which you
can see on the cover big letters spelling out "Henry James,"
but not the full title of the particular volume.

I remember having lingered over that photo when I first
saw it. And I remember noticing the distinctive patterning in
the railing when reading, a year or so earlier, one biography
it appeared in. It is painted green, I see now. And I assure
myself that I have logged some real progress in covering the
city, or at least the central pocket of it (metropolitan Buenos
Aires at twelve million inhabitants is simply huge, going on
for miles), if I can stumble on something like this ironwork
and in a way recognize it. I tell myself that the moment probably marks for this trip the important pivot point in any trip,
when the foreign country doesn't feel *so* foreign anymore.
That's nice, too.

I eat a lot of steak on the trip, because *carne* (the word
seems synonymous with "steak" in Argentina) is indeed the

country's staple. Nevertheless, even at my size, six-two, I can only handle what they call a *mini-bife* and not the thick, plate-size slab the average slim Argentine male is able to put away daily at lunch with no hesitation. There's an awful lot of pizza and pasta, too, evidence of how Italian Buenos Aires really is, with Italian immigration having been very large and possibly more Italian than Spanish last names in the city phone book today, I think I read somewhere. There are also big street demonstrations going on pretty much daily all over town during the whole time I am here. They attract me at first, an opportunity to be maybe a Witness to History in this period of the country's huge economic upheavals, now that the government has let the peso float entirely freely (without much buoyancy, by the way), but the street marches are inevitably played out to guys setting off ear-splitting firecrackers. After a couple of bursts igniting only a matter of yards from my tympanic membranes, I learn my lesson, and I don't follow the crowds when I see the demonstrations building.

6. Café Richmond, Calle Florida, 6 P.M.

What proves to be another minus on the metaphysical chart, but a revealing sequence, nevertheless.

This particular afternoon I decide to go into the Café Richmond on Calle Florida. Apparently, Borges, a regular, would bring visiting scholars and journalists there when they sought him out in the city, not far from the Calle Maipú apartment; it seems he let just about anybody who showed up at his door interview him. I admit I would not venture into the Richmond if it weren't for the Borges connection, and with gleaming brass pillars out front and abundant staid wood paneling visible behind the glass exterior there on the ritzy shopping concourse that is Calle Florida, it looks like an overpriced, somewhat official landmark of the sort that it's just a given you should avoid. Like Deux-Magots in Paris. And in front of the Richmond, I maybe smile to remember how Richard Ford, a predictable writer who many critics tend to take too seriously, once commented that he liked to write in a Paris café, but *never* Deux-Magots—as if he had some insider's knowledge that Deux-Magots is nowadays by and large terminally square, which anybody who *really* knows Paris merely takes for granted. And to think about Ford's straightforward, easily marketable writing is somehow to remind myself how it is typical of the kind of cookie-cutter fare that currently rules the American fiction scene, so much safe realism displaying no real verbal and structural daring, let alone transporting vision; possibly that American fiction scene is *deservedly* Oprah-ized. And I maybe think that part of losing myself in this whole Borges obsession is probably to ultimately remind myself what matters in writing, in art itself; an uncompromising and risk-taking career like that of Borges—by every account always a modest, unassuming man, even if he could turn noisy with his occasional awkwardly conservative politics—*is* something worthwhile in being obsessed with.

The Richmond inside spreads huge, a cavernous expanse of tables, with some businessmen unwinding, ditto for the women having finished a day of shopping and the few couples in low conversation here and there. Downstairs, where I have taken a look, it is livelier, an equally big expanse and well-heeled citizens playing billiards and chess, all male there. The waiter struts over to me, and in my Spanish that I am getting more confident with daily, I tell him I don't need the menu. I say I will just have the *promoción* for five pesos, which includes a *chopp* (draft) of beer and a plate of canapés; I saw it advertised on a placard outside, it seeming one item that will spare me from a gouging. As he walks off, I remind him again, too loudly, *"La promoción por cinco pesos."* Mustached, gray-haired, dignified, he simply waves my addendum away, as if to say, "Yes, yes, I heard you." I realize that going on with my talk of a *promoción*, which loosely translates as "sale" or "special," wasn't the classiest of lines. What the hell.

The British long dominated Argentina's economy, and Borges's grandmother on his father's side was from the U.K. Looking around the Richmond you are reminded how British (alternating with the Italian feel) Argentina can be, if only for a certain upper-crust sort, and the Richmond—paintings of British ocean liners and busy British fox hunting on the walls—is *very* British during the tea hour, much more so than even the other trappings around B.A. I've seen so far (the polo-gear store, the British-style parks, Harrods), granting that the Falklands War dampened most overt Anglo enthusiasm. If there is no metaphysic oozing through the comfortably frigid air conditioning this late afternoon, there is for me a better understanding of Borges's British side—how he loved the literature of Kipling and Stevenson and Chesterton throughout his life, how some members of the higher class like him, with British connections, supported the Allies in the Second World War, while many Argentines remained somewhere between neutral and openly backing the Axis powers of Nazi Germany and fascist Italy.

The waiter brings the beer, golden and cold, and a sizable stainless-steel plate bearing the fancy canapés, the ones with chunks of fish in the puffed pastry the best. I take my time with it all. I decide I actually like it in here, the Café Richmond.

7. Did I Tell You I *Saw* Borges?

Which, of course, is a trick line. And, rest assured, I'm not going to announce something totally wacky. I'm not going to claim I had a vision of Borges reincarnated and strolling around—walking cane in hand, as he was often photographed when older—in the city those summer days of such hot, honey sunshine.

No, this happened when I was in college. Borges came to Harvard to give the Charles Eliot Norton Lectures in Poetry in 1967. A sophomore English major, I wasn't as sophisticated in matters literary as my roommate, Dan Sorensen, who enthusiastically told me that Borges was the new giant on the scene, easily as important as Beckett, and that I *had* to accompany him to see the man in Sanders Theatre. Not that Dan was absolutely sophisticated, and he had come to Cambridge from a high school in suburban Salt Lake City; that at least had the edge, I guess, on my education at an unknown private boys' school in Rhode Island at the hands of, often literally, an order of black-robed Catholic brothers, the whole package quite medieval. I remember having dinner in the Quincy House dining room and then heading along the snow-shoveled sidewalks (the sidewalks of Cambridge frequently being snow-shoveled in my memory—or in my dreams) to one of the lectures. We filed into the Victorian teacup that is Sanders Theatre, to sit high up; we watched ushered onto the stage a partially blind (read "Homeric") man in a black suit, grinning. Whatever he lectured about I am not sure today, to be frank, though the look alone of him in that black suit, grinning some more and speaking softly and somewhat unintelligible even with a microphone, his longish, thinning silver hair combed straight back, has always lingered in my mind as the image of the Poet as archetype, or "Ur-poet," a figure representative of the full wisdom that literature, when it is *great* literature, truly can be. I read a lot of Borges after that, as everybody did in the sixties, the peak of his popularity, and then I came back to him later in life after writing for some time myself, with a new intensity, with a new appreciation, too, of the craft and vision of what he did in those fully innovative, dazzling short stories. More recently I read my way through the poetry, finding there a large body of work that can, surprisingly, hold its own with the stories. So I did once see Borges.

I suppose I have other Borges links as well. I live in Austin and teach at the university there now, and Borges came with his mother to University of Texas to teach in 1961–62 as a visiting professor, loving the town. I even think I have pretty good evidence that a late Borges short story, "The Bribe," about an encounter between a young Turk of a scholar and an Old English professor in the professor's office at UT, takes place in the very building where I work, Parlin Hall, home of the Department of English, though Borges doesn't name it; Borges himself was in residence under the auspices of the Department of Spanish and Portuguese when at the university, so his own office must have been in their building.

Connections that are good to think about, probably meaning nothing and not especially strange. But what *was* strange was what happened when I set out on the trip, maybe nearly as weird as any actual sighting of Borges back in the flesh in B.A.

A creative writing grad student of mine gave me a lift to the airport in his maroon pickup. I had gotten out of the truck, was yanking my single small bag from the front seat (I've learned to travel supremely light), and he said:

"Pete, look."

"What?"

"Look—that guy sitting there."

In mid-afternoon, the drop-off/pick-up concourse in front of the sprawling new terminal was virtually empty, save for a college-age guy sitting on a concrete slab of a bench; a suitcase beside him, he was waiting for a taxi or bus, sure-ly—*and* reading a copy of Borges's *Labyrinths*, its distinctive black-and-white glossy cover showing a blurred photograph of superimposed abstract blocks, almost a maze. It was the *only* complete literary "text" I myself had packed in my own bag, along with a Lonely Planet travel guide and a Spanish dictionary, plus those photocopies of a couple dozen Borges poems. Or look at it this way—I was going to Buenos Aires to see if I could indeed savor some of Borges's metaphysic, and sitting there as I was about to depart was a guy in a tur-tleneck reading a copy of *Labyrinths*, the book that contains a good chunk of his major work.

I mean, think of all the airports in the world. Think of all the books in the world. Think of all the different hours and minutes in all the different time zones in the world. A coincidence, perhaps, but, again, what are the sheer odds of a guy happening to be sitting there at that exact moment when I crossed paths with him and reading the book by Borges that I had brought for no other reason than I just wanted to feel what it was like to do some reading of the man in Argentina, "on the premises," so to speak?

I like to think Borges would have loved it.

But to get back to my time in Buenos Aires.

8. The Worst Job in the World

I'm in the subway, going to a stop far out on this, the "E" line. I'm on my way to the Biblioteca Municipal Miguel Cané at the end of Calle Carlos Calvo, well beyond downtown.

It's a Friday afternoon, hot enough on the street above and a bona fide inferno down in the subway, my shirt soaked with sweat. When Borges conceded that he had to bring in an income more steady than what his literary journalism (of which he turned out a sizable amount) provided him, he landed, through the help of friends, an appointment as an "assistant" at this small Buenos Aires neighborhood library in 1937. He was thirty-eight, rather old, admittedly, to find a first real job; he was there for nine years. The employment was painful, a long tram ride back then to a distant and bleak part of town for him. He himself writes in his "Autobiographical Essay" about it, and the biographers document the experience well. His fellow employees were mostly loafers who had gotten their jobs as political plums, guys who talked about soccer and women the entire day. When Borges worked a little too fast at the task of cataloguing all the books there according to the Dewey Decimal system, a major project underway, his coworkers called him aside and told him something along the lines of, "Whoa, Trigger"—if everybody did that much work every day, half of them would be canned before long because there would be nothing to do. Borges apparently became very upset, understandably, about a rape that occurred in the ladies' room, off the main reading room, yet his coworkers told him that it was only inevitable, considering the way that somebody had foolishly, in their opinion, built the ladies' room right next to the men's room in the library (worse, I seem to recall reading that the prime suspect turned out to be a *fellow librarian*). In the honored tradition of many government employees, Borges soon learned to lose himself in personal projects on state time, carefully studying *The Divine Comedy* in Italian, writing his own work. Borges was a vocal critic of Colonel Juan Domingo Perón and the latter's rise to power after World War II, and when the man did assume the presidency in 1946, Borges received official word from the Peronista administration that while he would keep a government job, he was being transferred to a position as chief inspector of poultry and rabbits at the Calle Córdoba public marketplace (Borges's own version of the incident). It was surely seen as a hilarious joke to be played on somebody they thought to have ties to the smug—and for them hated and overtly elitist—oligarchy. When faced with the poultry-inspecting job, Borges had no choice but resign. True, Borges often spoke about how distasteful working at the Biblioteca Municipal Miguel Cané was, qualifying it for any list of the most legendary bad jobs in literary history, ranked right up there with Dickens's time as a child in the blacking factory. And, as I said, I'm on the subway now heading there, the heat in the un-air-conditioned car itself dead with that smell of vacuum cleaner innards that all subways possess.

Once above terra firma, I see a neighborhood of mostly new apartment buildings that today doesn't seem that bad, and at least there flows a slight breeze. The Biblioteca Municipal Miguel Cané is a white two-story rise with the standard Neoclassical masonry decoration (grape leaves, bunting), looking quite like that house where Borges was born, and outside is another plaque, here giving the dates of Borges's employment as a librarian. Inside, the first impression is that everything is more or less in a time buckle, that the place probably hasn't changed much whatsoever since Borges served his sentence here. On the first floor there's a reading room with dark-wood tables and chairs, a row of tall, dark-wood bookcases dividing it in two. The holdings appear to be what you would expect in a neighborhood library—some popular fiction (I notice John Grisham in translation), some encyclopedias, a hefty red-bound Merck Manual. In one of my Borges-territory guidebooks I have seen a snapshot that gives evidence that despite Borges's own public proclamation of distaste for the place, there is now a little room they have set up for a display with apparently his desk and chair from his working days here; or, as the caption with the picture in the book would have it: "...*un sillón y un pupitre utilizados por Borges cuando trabajada allí*." That is my target of sorts for today. A wiry guy in brown jeans and a short-sleeve beige shirt, rumpled, approaches me; his skin is leathery, his slicked-back black hair sparse, his mustache what they used to call pencil-thin. Fifty or so, gruff, he doesn't strike you as your typical librarian, and when I spout off something about looking for "*un sillón y un pupitre utilizados por Borges*," he appears to only pick up on the "Borges" part of it.

"Jorge Luis Borges?" he says, not excited about it.

"*Sí, sí*," I say.

He leads me to a small bookcase in the rear of the room; here they have, alongside some ancient classics of Spanish literature in flaking calfskin bindings, a set of the blue-bound complete works of Borges. He hands me the volume containing the poems, while he doesn't say anything about where I might find "*un sillón y un pupitre utilazados por Borges.*" To be polite, I sit down at one of the long tables, thumb through the book. I also look around, the overhead fans churning through the degrees centigrade, and the heat here is just about the same as in the subway. Dirty pale green walls; high ceilings with embossing; up front a single, cheesy turned-off computer on a table, next to a small bookcase of videotapes—those two items attesting that things have at least changed *some* since Borges's days at the library. And, of course, there in back are two doors side by side: "*Damas*" and "*Caballeros*," the scene of the crime. The mustached guy is ignoring me, so I now try a woman at the front desk, forty-something with heavy lipstick, hennaed hair, and a red dress. I hate to say it, but she looks a lot more like a hooker than any of the authentic examples I eventually took notice of around the classy San Martín quarter downtown. I give her the line about my trying to find "*un sillón y un pupitre utilaza-dos por Borges,*" and she talks to me while sitting on a stool and thumbing through a stack of dog-eared index cards that are yellow-going-to-brown with age. She finally looks up, telling me to wait a minute, and after she walks off and disappears from the reading room to go to maybe the office of the head librarian in back, the mustached guy getting summoned in there, too, the mustached guy eventually comes out on his own, heading toward me up front and carrying a ring of keys; saying nothing, he just casually motions me to follow him upstairs. I do. We cross a gallery area up there, and he takes me to an addition in back. He unlocks the door to a closet-sized, windowless nook, where they have set up the display. I walk in, start taking some notes about the look of the desk (which really seems like just the same type of long table I saw in the reading room, with three upright dividing boards to make three small carrels, an attached reading lamp above each section) and the chair (a bentwood one with arms and a too-new, red leatherette cushion); there are some mounted newspaper clips about Borges on the desk and old schoolbook copies in Spanish of the stories of Oscar Wilde and *Tales from Shakespeare* by Charles and Mary Lamb, yet I'm not sure exactly what they have to do with B., whether he contributed translations or if they were just his personal copies. There are some photographs of him when young. I take more notes, glance outside once.

In the corridor, the mustached guy has found a ledge to sit on, low and hunched over. His chin on one fist, he has lit up a cigarette and is puffing it slowly, flicking the ashes to the floor, then puffing it slowly some more. I suspect that he is thinking, "I wonder how long this crazy American bastard is going to be in there," but maybe he is grateful for having to conduct the tour, getting the windfall of this unexpected smoking break. Also, I hate to say it, but he, too, could have been a leftover—very much so—from when Borges was employed here, one of those rowdy guys talking only of women and soccer. But he does finally smile, politely, when I finish and thank him for his time, his locking up again with the big ring of keys, and I feel foolish for thinking what I had about him.

Downstairs, I sit alone at the same table again, taking more notes. There are a couple of men there, senior citizens, reading books at other tables. A college-age girl in camouflage pants and black T-shirt appears to be doing an assignment. A woman with a baby cradled in one arm comes in and the librarian in the red dress helps her look up something. I'm really hot, hotter than when I was in the subway. I take still more notes. I notice the girl in camouflage pants get up and bounce toward the ladies' room in back, and I can't *help* but think again myself of the odious crime that once transpired right there. I'm really, really hot, the shirt glued to my back again, and looking out the old story-high front doors with glass panels and to the street, I see the leaves on a jacaranda rattling, so I know there remains somewhat of a breeze out there. I want to be out there, escape, and I tell myself, yeah, I am getting a taste of the experience of what it was like for Borges. I think of jobs I had when younger that I hated, clock-watching jobs and most of them involving what for me was the day-to-day, repetitive grind of city newspaper work, before I was downright lucky enough to find teaching positions in creative writing. I get up to leave. I thank the woman in the red dress at the front desk, and she also finally smiles, as I feel foolish for having thought ill of her, too.

I know I still have the Biblioteca Nacional to go to before I leave Buenos Aires.

In a fitting reversal of fortune right after Perón was deposed in 1955, Borges, who had been supporting himself with university teaching and editing since leaving the assistant's post at the neighborhood library, was appointed by the new government the director of the national library, an institution that is the equivalent of our Library of Congress. It was a prestigious position that, from every report, he deeply loved for the almost twenty years he held it, until resigning in 1973, when an embalmed-looking Perón returned from exile in Spain for a brief final term in office before officially dying. By then B.'s worldwide notoriety (the French were the first to celebrate him abroad, as they have been in the cases of so many writers slighted in their homelands) led to constant international travel with lucrative lecturing and major prizes, which, along with substantial book sales, rendered him financially independent. He accepted his increasing blindness, an inherited affliction.

9. Reading and Thinking at Night

Still dressed in chinos, a loose chambray shirt with the sleeves rolled up, and comfortable Reeboks, I'm stretched out on my made bed at the Hotel Phoenix. I am reading an interesting little book I came across in a used bookstore, a tattered paperback history of the Argentine short story published in 1975. I have bought a couple of tallboy cans of Brahma beer at a corner *kiosco* (deli), drinking one now while reading, keeping the other cool by having wrapped it in a heavy white terrycloth bath towel. It's *ultimately* interesting how in that two-hundred-page survey of the genre, Borges merits only a little more than two pages, and even then he is unceremoniously lumped together in a roundup for a chapter titled, "*Cuentistas que no figuran en las antologías Argentinas del cuento*," or the writers who at that time hadn't made it into the standard anthologies of the Argentine short story. The author, a certain Carlos Mastrángelo, talks of the difficulty of Borges's stories, albeit respectfully, while most of the book is concerned with what he seems to believe is the country's more noteworthy fare, much of it work in what could be called the "gaucho tradition," by local-colorists, really. Nevertheless, I am drinking the Brahma in its sweating white-and-red tallboy can, wondering why Borges by 1975 didn't get anthologized, unless ignoring him was possibly a political thing and Borges for some Argentine critics was simply out of the loop on that count, therefore afforded scant publicity. I get up to unwrap the second Brahma from the towel, and I feel it in my grip—it is still very cold.

All the doors to the three balconies are open now, and there is a breeze, slowly lifting then dropping the long maroon drapes gently, as if they are breathing. The latest round of overdramatic thunderstorms that afternoon has finally cleared out the air, and around town in the last couple of days I've seen school kids in uniforms returning to the start of fall classes; the season is changing. Going out to the center, corner balcony above the major downtown intersection, I look to the wedge of the glassy black river a few blocks away, tall yellow cranes at the docks framing the view; there is a moon, full. I sip the cold Brahma. The night smells muddily sweet, if that makes any sense, and I am at that last stage in a trip when you start missing things already. I know I will miss this giant room, the best in the old, well-worn hotel, so maybe it *was* where the Prince of Wales himself stayed. I will miss eating those good steaks and not worrying about blood pressure and cholesterol, because, as I tell myself at the table every day, "You'll only be in Argentina once, Pete." I'll even miss goofing around with the group of Australian women at breakfast. Just that morning, Brendie (in a tight top displaying a lot of peachy cleavage, as usual) was giving me more commentary on the tango, with her pal named Georgia noddingly agreeing. Brendie said: "The tango really freed the poor here. It struck some rhythm in them that made them forget their sadness for a while." The whole of which could have been trite, a platitude, until Brendie added, talking more to herself than anybody else: "There's so much sadness that people need to forget." Brendie is OK. Despite any early doubts about the trip (those fears of indulging in too much self-examination concerning my admitted mess-ups in life), I realize that this is turning out to be one of the best trips I've taken in a long while, probably since going to India and especially Bombay, which was something else, too. (I traveled around for a month to give some lectures in India, had a great time with the bright and wonderfully energetic Indian students while in residence as a visiting faculty member at an American studies research center in Hyderabad; it was a place where everybody was wild about books—long informal sessions with the students late into the night, talking literature, long walks with them to the dusty hills behind the center's compound in the afternoons, talking literature. And then a week in shimmering, forever mysterious Bombay, a major world city on par with London or Paris or New York, I tell myself now.) I guess I'm also thinking of everything I have to do back in Austin. I have to plow through the chore of really complicated income taxes this year, and though I am on official academic leave now for a semester, there's waiting for me back home the ongoing baloney that can surround academia sometimes. Not from the students, who are great, but from vapidly self-important administrators, "politic, cautious, and meticulous," and lately such campus careerists can even be found on the creative writing end, another sign of the dim and commercialized literary times. But one must keep loudly bucking the likes of them, try to make things better, also always try to instill in graduate creative writing students specifically, I remind myself now, a hunger for the *lasting and significant,* the old Borgesian ethos, all right. On the balcony, I tell myself that a duration of a couple of weeks in my adult life is about as long as I can go without working on my own fiction, and I admit I'm jumpy to get back to that, already planning new projects. I go inside again. I stretch out on the bed again, continue reading the paperback history of the Argentine short story.

10. Thinking Some More at Night

And from the bed I can see myself reflected—me, comfortably tired after walking, relaxing like that with book in hand, the ceiling fan above lopsidedly looping around and around—in the full-length mirror on the huge mahogany armoire with its tarnished brass fittings. That reminds me again of that Borges museum, which was empty except for the single round mirror left to reflect people passing by on the busy sidewalk of Calle Tucumán, or reflect a stranger like me cupping my hands at twilight there to look in—Borges himself long gone but the mirror still *very much* around. Borges was right to be suspicious of mirrors, and often it's easy to feel that not much of anything is close to what we commonly call real.

I sip the beer. I continue with the book on the history of the Argentine short story.

11. Brendie Says

The next morning at breakfast I ask Brendie if maybe she knows what the deal is on those tourism maps, how north is south and south is north. Is it because the layout of the city just fits better on the page that way? Or, possibly, is it because we're below the Equator, and it's like the sink draining the other way? Is it the same on maps in Australia? Pretty and practical Brendie, the physical therapist, pauses in her spooning the cornflakes into her lipsticked mouth (the Hotel Phoenix harbors Anglo airs), and she says she hasn't noticed it, adding with a grin, "Don't be daft—of course maps aren't that way in Australia." Perfect.

12. Books as Pure as Air Itself

The former Biblioteca Nacional is on Calle México, number 564, in a funky district of older, colonial-style architecture called Barrio Sur, south of the Plaza de Mayo. It's siesta time, early afternoon, hot again but without the humidity, and the streets here are all but deserted—or more than that, everything is perfectly and utterly still. I see the high façade rising above the low houses around it on narrow Calle México, flat granite lower down and a row of six huge pillars above that, like a proud old American bank, imposing; however, as I already know, it is no longer the Biblioteca Nacional, granting the Roman lettering chiseled in the top peak's triangle still announces exactly that. The library has been moved to a new venue of reinforced-concrete brutalist architecture—pretty ugly—in an outlying park, and now the former library serves as a national music center, with performance space and offices for administration. As a cultural seat, therefore, it hasn't escaped the recent protest that is currently questioning any elitism in Argentina—financial, cultural, or otherwise—and in swirly spray-painting, red and black, on the walls near the sidewalk you can read:

"ATACA EL ESTADO!"
and:

"COLONIALES!'
and:
"EL SECTOR DE LOS MESÍAS LOCOS!"

The first two needing no translation or commentary, and the last identifying the music center as another operation of the crazy messiahs, who I assume are the allegedly corrupt government bigwigs who are charged with landing the country in the current economic mess. If nothing else, it's free of the particular graffiti that blankets just about every bank building downtown: "LADRONES!" Thieves.

The tall carved-wood front doors are open, and I head up the granite steps. It's cooler in the expanse of the foyer, tiled with squares in a red-and-yellow floral pattern. A slim young guy in black slacks and a white open-neck shirt but no hat, his security uniform, is at the desk, very soft-voiced and friendly. After he seems assured that I am not mistaken that this is the present seat of the national library and understand that it is now the music center, he affirms that it once was, in fact, the Biblioteca Nacional, and that Borges indeed was the director. I ask him if I can look around, and he tells me of course I can, ushering me through a set of high doors to what had been the central reading room. He leaves me alone there, goes back to his desk in the lobby, deserted like everywhere else, it seems, during a weekday siesta time.

The place is wonderful.

I am standing alone in the middle of an octagonally shaped empty space, five stories high. The floor is planked; each level above me is ringed by a gallery walkway, with doorways at the corners showing very intricately carved trim; there are long plaques listing the great names of "*Ciencia*," "*Filosofía*,"

and such in gold (Plato, Herodotus, etc.); the walls themselves are all bookshelves and paneling, the fine, aged wood-
work the color of walnut; up top is a domed skylight, and
in the middle of that is what looks like a Tiffany-glass insert
with huge stars in an indigo-blue night sky (harking back
to the building's original intended use, as a center for the
government lottery—the stars of luck?). A stage has been set
up in front, for recitals, but it still feels entirely like a reading
room, and a magnificent one at that. I think of Borges's short
story "The Library of Babel," about a mythical library where
books endlessly lead to still more books about those books,
then books about those books about those books, and so on,
a dizzying, infinite maelstrom of verbal information that
maybe foretold the computer age. And while nearly every
commentator on the story, including Borges himself, noted
that its inspiration traced back to the seemingly endless cataloguing travail when Borges worked at Biblioteca Municipal
Miguel Cané, I remember that in his "Library of Babel" the
rooms of the imagined library are six-sided, giving a spiraling
sense of continuity—that touch surely must have been influenced by the time he spent here in the course of his life, as
far back as when he had first visited the library as a schoolboy
poring over the *Encyclopaedia Britannica*. And it's *so* quiet in
here. Of course, I'm back to taking notes. I'm also thinking
how it is pleasant to picture Borges finally having "arrived"
in his native land, the lord of this domain, when it suddenly
hits me: *There is everything here for a library but the books—the
shelves are completely and achingly empty.* It deals me a measure
of near vertigo even greater than that from having seen the
mirror in the museum, and I sense for a moment maybe the
ultimate idea of books, the purity of the thoughts and the

knowledge, often the veritable transcendence, they convey, all of which in a way isn't the least bit corporeal; it is one message certainly at the center of Borges's basic credo. (Stories like "The Library of Babel," or "The Approach to al-Mu'Tasim," a fiction in the form of an imaginary review of an imaginary book, or "Pierre Menard, Author of the *Quixote*," where an obsessed contemporary man tries to rewrite the Cervantes masterpiece by virtually becoming Cervantes—learning his seventeenth-century Spanish, schooling himself in the ways of Cervantes's own day—to the point that he does eventually sit down to rewrite it, but as himself now, Pierre Menard, and the product is exactly the same *Don Quixote*, which shows how invisible, but enduringly constant, any book is in the mind, almost beyond and independent of the author.) The *physical absence* of books here is somehow the *magical essence* of books. And for me in the Biblioteca Nacional, mark a hole-in-one, a perfectly pitched game, a ninety-yard run, whatever, on the Scoreboard of Metaphysical Moment.

When I walk out to the foyer, the young guy hands me a brochure on the music center, which will be good to have for future reference because it does contain color photos and a floor plan of the building. I tell him Borges interests me very much and that I am, though *definitely* not in the league of Borges, an "*escritor norteamericano*" myself. He nods, smiles. I walk back out into empty Calle México. When I return the next afternoon to take another look, check some things for my notes, the young attendant comes into the reading room to talk to me a little. He asks me in his soft voice if what I said is true, that I am an "*escritor norteamericano*."

I tell him yes, repeating that I am very interested in Borges. He tells me that others are, too. I ask him if people come every day, and he says not every day, but they come *often* for a look. Then he looks at me, and says in his Spanish, serious:

"An American writer, that is a good thing to be."

I thank him, feeling good about that myself, while knowing I seldom introduce myself as any kind of writer at all—I have managed to publish a few books of fiction, but I must admit that I usually feel a complete interloper in claiming to be a *real* writer (no need to dive noggin-first into that particular lack of assurance or soul-searching here).

I leave Buenos Aires a day later, totally enamored with the city, a *most* complicated one, and deeply hoping, as well, that Argentina tugs itself out of its financial quagmire soon—the place is too special for that sort of stuff.

13. Where I Really Am

Needless to say, where I really am is here in my apartment at 1407 West 39th ½ Street in Austin, Texas.

It is Easter, March 29, 2002, and earlier I went to a seven-thirty Mass, had breakfast, then returned here to get back to work on this piece, the computer screen glowing. Since I've been back in Austin, I've been alternating working on this with working on a long short story set in Buenos Aires, "Southern Majestic Zone," which is going really well. Now and then I slip a CD of orchestra tango classics—the thumping *bandoneon* accordion, the sighing violins—into the computer's player for mood while I write; I have maps and notes and the books bought on my trip spread out on the carpet around my desk. Naturally, I hope that for anybody reading this it has felt as if *you* were actually with me in Buenos Aires, and I can say (here comes the shameless Borgesian imitation, pulling out

the rug from under the wobbling guise of reality in the artifice in order to dispose of any pretension to such easy reality
in the artifice, as the narrative hopefully evokes and enters
into some yet *higher* reality *well beyond* artifice; but in this case
I probably blew it a while ago when I awkwardly abandoned
present tense for past in the section that moved back toward
my remembering seeing Borges in person at Sanders Theatre
at Harvard that cold late November night), yes, I can say that
writing it, I truly felt I was in the moment, actually there.

Believe me, my flimsy initial premise for the trip didn't
backfire after all, and I think I did tune in on (be a son of
the sixties and be forever shackled to its loopy jargon) the
metaphysic in all my rereading of Borges there, in all my
tramping around town and playing the old, and thoroughly
exciting, literary fan's game of following in the footsteps
there. The place was *laced* with metaphysic, if you know
what I mean.

14. On the Other Hand

I get up to take a break from writing, stroll around my bed-
room/study. I walk to the large sliding-glass doors and look
out beyond the second-floor deck at what should be my
neighbors' sun-splashed, fenced-in backyard with its uncut
emerald grass and its dog pen for the obnoxious, neurotic
golden lab and its clutter of kids' bicycles…and, no kidding, I
seem to be much higher up, I seem to have a balcony view of
Avenida Córdoba in Buenos Aires, busy with horn-blowing
taxis right down to the docks and those tall yellow cranes
there, where the Plata is now strikingly silver and not its
usual cinnamon tone as the noontime sunlight hits it just the
right way, living up to its name.

That's what I'm looking at.
No kidding, that's what I see!

15. (And 16, 17, 18, 19, etc.) Plus, What About?

Plus, if you don't follow me on that, what about that kid who was sitting like a statue there outside the airport, reading *Labyrinths*, something that has to go well beyond mere coincidence? I mean, *you* tell *me*.

2004, FROM *AGNI MAGAZINE*

THE CITY AT THREE P.M.: AN ESSAY ON WRITING

1.

The bars on Ninth Avenue are empty in the warm October sunshine. Walking the grimed sidewalk and passing the narrow cross streets, you can look down any one of them and right across the fragilely blue Hudson, to the other side and New Jersey, where the trees have already turned to pastels—soft red, soft yellow. If you are walking around rather aimlessly at this hour, taking a break during a full day of writing, you could do what you have done before. You could work your way over to Broadway and Times Square, cutting up Forty-third Street to look at the Hotel Carter again. And the Hotel Carter is for some reason mesmerizing, if only for the fact that just the other day you discovered that it had once been called the Dixie Hotel. The Dixie Hotel was where poor Delmore Schwartz was living when he returned to New York in 1966, half mad and broken in his last days, after all the early success and adulation from even the likes of T.S. Eliot. Once-handsome Schwartz, the poet of such sweeping blond hair and a matinee idol's high cheekbones when young, was by that point physically as well as artistically spent, strung out on alcohol and pills and convinced the CIA was plotting against him, before he died of a massive coronary at the age of fifty-two (not in the Dixie but another Times Square hotel?) while taking garbage from his cramped room out to the steel-grated back landing; the body was unclaimed in the morgue for days, so the story goes. The Hotel Carter rises in a pile of beige brick, "Seven Hundred Rooms" the faint paint of the lettering touts high up on one side; it is flanked by closed-down shops that are all part of the maybe evil movie-industry conglomerate's plan to "rehabilitate" the area (literal Disneyfication), and across the street are the staid white lamp globes outside the Times Building. But it is too sunny, too warm, to just stand on the pavement and stare at the Hotel Carter again, think of the sadness at the end of a truly talented poet's life, think, too, about the larger question: How could anybody who knew so much about the way the heart works, in those poems and the handful of short stories, end up denied any soothing knowledge about anything, in so much pain? Which has often been the, yes, larger question, and you know you should probably avoid being anywhere near the Hotel Carter right now. On Ninth Avenue there is a bar called the Film Center Café. It has a streamlined chrome façade and blue neon sign, taking its name from the nearby Film Center Building, a genuine 1920s Art Deco behemoth with offices for assorted media and other enterprises now, though somebody once told you that years ago it actually was the very heart of the film industry in the city. You could go over to the café, a bar and restaurant setup, and talk to the tall, dark-haired girl from Newry in Northern Ireland who tends bar there. She has been in the States for only three months, lives in Astoria, and has a Northern Irish bartender boyfriend here in New York (they are Catholics); she plans to marry him soon, return to Northern Ireland with him. She is that rarest of entities, a true beauty without realizing it, wearing black turtlenecks and black jeans, also makeup and lipstick that she really doesn't need; her eyes are large and green. To talk to her is to tell her about your own time in Ireland years before when you lived in Dublin for a while and did some work as a journalist, and to talk to her is to have her always listen without pretense, because it is obvious she's relaxed with you, likes you, as she would a favorite uncle, maybe. And who else comes into the empty Film Center Café in the afternoon to say to her that, sure, she could be the only twenty-five-year-old girl in America who regularly goes to Mass, and who else listens to her go on about how all she wants to do is return to Ireland with her Sean: "I want to have a lot of babies, I suppose"? If most things in your life have to suggest some literary tie, then she is the quiet, level-headed, lovely Nora Barnacle whom Joyce married, so naive that when you ask her the population of her town, little Newry, she says in the lilt with a touch of Scottish flatness that is the Northern Ireland brogue, "A million, I would guess." So, to chat with her at the Film Center Café now at almost three in the afternoon would be to watch the sunlight streaming in through the unwashed windows, onto the dented mahogany bar, the authentically red-and-black checkered linoleum. It would be to think how lucky Joyce had been to realize early on that Nora Barnacle in her apparent, and deceptive, simplicity possessed a strength that he himself never really had, that she was very rare. But it is such a beautiful day, and being indoors at the Film Center Café might be as much of a mistake as gazing at the Hotel Carter again. You could always head up Ninth Avenue, eventually find yourself on Fifty-eighth Street, let's say, west of Central Park.

2.

What can startle you on a weekday afternoon is the sheer number of black limousines and executive town cars, chauffeur driven, in a pocket of the city like that. There are the usual posh apartment buildings, some baroque-trimmed and some more modern, and then the new offices, glass-and-steel high-rises, but on a scale much smaller than those in the heart of midtown. In fact, away from the main avenues, all of it contributes to a distinct eeriness, and maybe a certain calm, too, being so empty; the air smells half of damp masonry and half maybe the imagined aroma of tobaccoey leaves turning— imagined because it surely can't waft from the few scrawny sycamores planted in the neatly tailored sidewalk and ringed with fan-patterned, rather Parisian grates, their thin leaves uniformly gold. The street is shadowed and cool, but looking straight above, you see a sky that seems enameled, so blue you think that somebody is maybe trying to trick you and no sky is *that* blue. And along the no-parking-zone curbs, and in the alcoves for the stilled parking ramps where a day's parking can easily cost you nearly what you would pay for a decent motel room in any other American city, are the big cars. Some of them are genuine stretch models, Cadillacs with tinted windows and chrome grilles that manage to grin every Cadillac's richness and confidence and sense of superiority. Others are boxy Lincolns that, even without being stretched, offer an evening-carriage coziness, what makes them very good limousines indeed, and others are the inevitable Mercedes, the three-pointed star on the hood; to look at a Mercedes with that glossy, rock-hard enamel it has and the particular craftsmanship in the way the seams along the fenders and trunk blend so tightly, almost invisibly, is to know why the Germans for years made the best binoculars, the best cameras as well. True, it is a street of limousines. And in almost every one, there is sure to be a chauffeur sleeping. Because these are the men in dark suits whose job by definition is probably more waiting than driving, and how lucky they are to be dozing soundly in the sun-fading afternoon. So, you do walk along Fifty-eighth Street, and there are the parked cars of the many chauffeurs sleeping, the windows on the driver's side rolled down. They appear entirely content in their slumber, and it is enough to make you ask yourself when you yourself last had a night's sleep that was really deep, for theirs is *wonderful* sleeping; it is as if to sleep would be to be sure of everything that you were always very much unsure of, would be to know the atomic weight of all the elements on the ancient wall chart at school and to know the important poetry contained in the very names of the different clouds, *cumulonimbus*, or better, *cirrostratus*. In one car a chocolate-complexioned man in a gray suit leans his handsome head against the leather rest atop the seat, and close to him as you pass, you feel that you almost know what he is dreaming. Or you know the dream of the Latino man with a pockmarked face and dark sunglasses in another car, who isn't in New York City at all anymore. He is walking as a child down a red-dirt road in one of those Caribbean villages with a whispering name, San Pedro de los Caballeros or La Barranca; there in a tiny house of white stucco and a crumbling terracotta roof, the bougainvillea cascading, his brother, who died very young, is still strong and alive, his grandmother, who raised the two of them, is waiting there, too, able to tell him at last about his father, the stevedore he never knew, tell why his mother ran away with a Trinidadian fisherman not long after that, and how in her heart of hearts, the beautiful young mother didn't mean to abandon two young sons to be raised (lovingly, nevertheless) by their grandmother. It would be something like that, because sleep as sound as all these men are sleeping can only generate flowering benevolence, can only heal. But then you move on, leave the dreaming chauffeurs. You head back down Ninth Avenue in the warmth and you feel at last ready to return to the roomy subleased apartment you have taken for a few months while staying in New York, a place on West Fifty-fifth, where you wrote well that morning.

Return there to read, even write a few paragraphs more of the new short story, before dinner later on.

2000, FROM *CREATIVE NONFICTION*

PLASTICIZE YOUR DOCUMENTS: WITH G. FLAUBERT IN TUNISIA

Time is a tyranny to be abolished.
—FROM A PARISIAN MANIFESTO

1. The Whole Idea

Seeing that the whole idea of the trip this time, going to Tunisia, is to meditate some on Flaubert and hopefully get a feel for an Arab world country to use in some of my own fiction I'm working on, I check over again what I've selected for books to bring.

2. Books; or, the Implements of Travel

** A Penguin Classics paperback of Flaubert's *Salammbô*, to reread. It's a novel often seen as the odd offering in his oeuvre, a lushly written near epic about ancient Carthage that has been controversial since the day it was published in 1862. I had some trouble finding a copy here in my home base of Austin, Texas, and with drives to the endless malls connected by the endless looping freeways, a configuration that defines sprawling Austin, I would go into another Barnes & Noble or Borders. At the "F" section in fiction I'd always hit a lot of Fannie Flagg but not much Gustave, outside of *Madame Bovary*, anyway. But I "scored"—that's the way it felt by that point—this Penguin Classics edition at a Borders far north in the subdivisioned city at last, translated by a certain A.J. Krailsheimer. It has a buff-and-black cover bearing the insert of an oil painting of a naked, flowing-haired young woman in a chamber of variegated marble pillars, a large flat-headed serpent upright like a cane beside her. The image is identified as being taken from "La Scène du Serpent" by Gaston Bussière, and doubtless it's Salammbô herself, the ethereally beautiful Carthaginian princess.

I tell myself it will be easy enough to pick up a cheap paperback of the book in French in Paris, where I will stop for a few days to see friends before going on to Tunis.

** This one deals me some sadness, an edition of Saint Augustine's *Confessions* printed in 1962. The small, mass-market-sized paperback has a cover like a stained-glass window, with an introduction by a Jesuit. The sadness is not in the 45-cent paperback itself with flaking yellowing pages, but how when I open it I see a signature in pencil on the title page. The signature is that of Ann McCabe. It's a name I haven't thought of in maybe forty years and who I now remember as my second oldest sister's roommate at the supposedly posh Order of the Sacred Heart college in a Boston suburb (the Kennedy girls were products of Sacred Heart boarding schools and colleges), an institution now long defunct. I knew the Saint Augustine was somewhere around my apartment in a box of accumulated books, and I found it and decided to take it along because he talks of being educated in Carthage when it became a Roman metropolis; Carthage, actually, was the city of Saint Augustine's debauchery as a university student before his eventual reform. The book's connection with my upcoming travel isn't all that great, but, more practically, it's probably the only thing I have on hand—besides the travel guides I've bought—that has much to do with Tunisia, site of ancient Carthage. And that signature, a boxy girl's script: to see it—stare at it, really—conjures up all those sadnesses commonly associated with Time somehow represented in smug personification, inevitably and brutally passing without giving a damn about anybody else. I think about how a girl—toothy and scrub-cheeked, with a blond pageboy haircut, the way I seem to remember her from weekend visits with my sister to our home—was once forced by the ritzy nuns to plow through a book like this that she didn't particularly want to plow through, and what a task, an ordeal, it must have been for her. And what does any of that matter today, several decades later? I wonder if Ann McCabe is even *alive* today, something that certainly never crossed my mind before. My sister and I see each other only infrequently, due to geography (more sadness, because she is so dear to me), and I don't remember her mentioning Ann lately.

** I also photostat some pages from Francis Steegmuller's two-volume *Letters of Flaubert*, specifically the few that Steegmuller includes from the quick fact-finding tour to Tunisia Flaubert launched out on in April 1858; that trip is not to be confused with his more extensive travels some years earlier with fellow writer (and photographer) Maxime Du Camp, journeying through the Middle East proper. The letters from Tunisia don't give much info, but there is still a very raucous Flaubert, the incorrigible roué sampling prostitutes in the Medina and waking up the whole neighborhood with the racket of his sport, then going at his research out at the ruins of Punic Carthage—not far from Tunis—for fourteen hours a day; he bounces along on a flea-bitten mule in the heat, picks scorpions out of his sleeping roll at night, and *loves* every minute of it.

3. Two Versions of Academia

Also, besides gathering the books to bring, I figure I might tap some resources at U. of Texas where I teach—do some prep, if you will, by seeking out faculty in the field for tips, more reading suggestions, etc., which doesn't prove much help, as it turns out. A cheery, crew-cut guy, middle-aged, in a sport shirt and Bermuda shorts in the linguistics department—he has a travel poster of a white Tunisian village on his office door, is an authority on Arabic—invites me in while he pokes a plastic fork at a takeout lunch in a styrofoam box; he explains to me that Tunisia has been his obsession since he first left the Midwest and went there as a Peace Corps volunteer years ago. He talks to me of hotels as well as the pluses and minuses of bus versus train for getting around in the country, then produces a guidebook that I already have, shows me various cities on the map (I pretend the book is new to me); the guy is more than friendly. Next I phone a newly appointed younger assistant professor in the French department. I've been told she's the current authority at UT on North African literature in French; she's from France herself, has taught in Tunis. On the phone, she sounds serious and so sincere, the way assistant professors can sound so sincere, and in a soft, French-tinged voice she just keeps going on and on with some academic jargon describing a book on harems she used for a class she taught and how it emphasizes the significance of "the gaze" (the word is "in" lately with scholarly critics, I know); I find myself looking at my watch, wondering when the talk will end. I might be somebody who, luckily, snuck into academia by the back door as a creative writer, with no credentials other than my own very small pile of published fiction to qualify me, yet I know I learned my lesson early: I seldom—but that doesn't mean never—get much of anything genuinely *important* when asking a "colleague" (even though I use it myself, I dislike that word, its pomposity), or scholarly ones, anyway. That includes either of the two standard types represented here: the benevolent, happy-go-lucky Elks Club variety like the linguistics citizen or the diligent, eternal-grad-student variety like the woman in the French department caught up in "the gaze."

Not to say that both didn't seem essentially good, well-intentioned people, as most academics are.

4. Still More Sadness

Starting out for North Africa, I first put in a few days, alone, at what's left of my family's old summer place on the ocean in Narragansett, Rhode Island, then a few days more in Paris, where I have taught a couple of times and still have those close friends.

In Narragansett I walk around the land out on a grassy point, assess the most recent winter damage to the ramshackle (approaching tumbledown) wood-shingled white house with a lot of bedrooms that my father built for our family not long after the war. I hack down some of the grass with a sputtering rusted rotary lawnmower then go at the shrubs with hand clippers to at least make the place look reasonably presentable for another season, losing myself in

the sheer exhaustion of the physical work in the blowy sunshine of late May; most of the neighboring houses are
still closed for the winter. I try working on my own fiction, but realize I need a longer uninterrupted stretch for
that. I get a book on Delacroix (a contemporary of Flaubert, with many of the same interests, I figure) at the little town library in Narragansett. And at night when the
fog has set in, the horn at Beavertail Light moaning from
across the bay, I find myself reading it while sitting in
the crack-walled living room with its faded Winslow Homer prints and clamshell ashtrays, there in the big maroon
leather chair that was the favorite of my father, a lawyer
and a judge whose lifelong heroes were Jefferson, Lincoln, and Roosevelt—for the last of these he proudly cast
his own vote in the Electoral College while a member of
the Democratic State Committee as a young man. Placing
a cardboard coaster as a marker in the pages, I think of
how happy all of us were when I was young and we spent
summers here, an ongoing carnival that usually included
packing the house with freeloading friends of my sisters
and mine from school and college, all the serious croquet
and all the boisterous big meals at the dining table, that
sort of thing. But most everybody in my immediate family is either dead now or not interested in the place much
at all anymore. I also think of Flaubert, and though I surely "ain't he," as they say, I can't help but remember that
he was a middle-aged bachelor still staying and writing
at what amounted to his own family's country retreat at
Croisset on the Seine near Rouen, the oddball in the clan,
and maybe old J.-P. Sartre was right to call him, yes, "the
family idiot."

In Paris I book into a noisy but cheap hotel. It's not far from the slim pillar topped with the freshly gilded angel at the Place de la Bastille, a neighborhood where I once lived.

It's also not far from an apartment Flaubert kept in Paris as a *pied-à-terre* for use while in the city from Normandy, after he wrote *Madame Bovary* and when maybe he was working on *Salammbô*: 42, Boulevard du Temple. I take a walk over there. The building is a recently sandblasted, buff-stone Parisian rise with ornate trim and glossy blue doors; there's, oddly, a row of modern motorcycle showrooms nearby. Technically part of the Marais, the area is today thoroughly renovated and yuppified, but the basic look of Flaubert's building probably hasn't changed much since he made his seasonal visits to the city from Normandy. He came for admittedly pretty heady literary and high-society company, a routine quite different from that when he was writing without interruption in the legendary near solitary confinement of Croisset; that part of his life prompted Baudelaire to describe him as an artistically dedicated "monk" rather than any family idiot. Studying the building, I tell myself you *have* to hand it to the French, the way they have preserved Paris; also, I like to think again that possibly some work on *Salammbô* itself was, in fact, done right here, only yards away from where I'm standing.

One academic acquaintance who has told me many *very important* things over the years is Claude Lévy, the leading Saul Bellow scholar in France. He's a handsome, rather dashing character, a man older than me and recently retired, whose wife is a professional opera singer. He was my chairman when I taught at Université Paris X-Nanterre, on exchange, and one evening on this trip, in the honey twilight that lingers until almost ten in Paris in June, I go with him to listen to his wife sing, her getting top billing in a concert on Île Saint-Louis; the three of us have lunch the next day at their apartment. He actually grew up in the small Jewish community in Tunis, leaving to study at the Sorbonne when eighteen. At lunch, there comes a moment over the good, bloodily rare roast beef and the good, grapily tart red wine and the good—*very* good—conversation and laughing, when he turns more serious, admitting that he hasn't been back to Tunisia for years. Today it's no place for a Jew, Claude says, but he asks me to do something for him. He says that when he was kid in Tunis, his aunt had a little summer house on the shore just north of the city at La Goulette-Vieille, and he talks of how happy he was spending school vacations there. He seems a bit lost to remember it, treading water in his own reminiscing sadness, as lost as I was back in my family's summer place in Rhode Island. (Why do summer places do this to people, even a guy like me who can barely afford my share of the sky-high taxes on mine and am constantly railing about how it chews up a big chunk of my modest teacher's paycheck? Why do summer places bring this out in people?) He explains that the little commuter train that leaves downtown Tunis and crosses Lake Tunis, a large inland saltwater lagoon, then goes up the coast to suburban Carthage, has a stop at La Goulette-Vieille. As he speaks, his lovely opera-singer wife Lisa, younger, just silently looks at him, and it is a look that says she has seen this sadness in him before—this expression of *utter* loss.

"You will see it," he tells me vacantly, perhaps trying to picture it himself. "Just look out the window, down the street of the village that leads to the sea. The house isn't there, but you will see where it was. Right at the end of the street. You know, why don't you stop there, visit it for me." From across the table he looks right at me. I can tell that this is something very important to him.

And I pronounce, cavalierly, decidedly Gallic style: "I certainly will!"

Finally, the next afternoon, I get out of the Air France jet in the bone-dry, ninety-degree June glare of Tunis. After booking into what seems a businessman's hotel called the Omrane, I later walk around some in the fine, white city, its wide main Avenue Bourguiba lined with box-cut trees and alive with sidewalk cafés, the melody-meandering Arab pop music playing everywhere. I feel the relief—even the sweet rush—of arrival that comes after you have spent altogether too much time jumping ahead of yourself and thinking about an upcoming trip, planning it, instead of just letting it happen—letting the first sights simply rise like some stumbled-upon dreamscape you always *suspected* was there but never were convinced would actually materialize, to dazzle you with the dreamlike texture that all travel, especially travel alone, certainly is. In a cubbyhole restaurant on Rue du Caire that evening, I eat what might be described as, well, "the best fucking couscous of my life" (the tomato sauce of it tangy, and the big bowl of semolina containing not only the usual carrots and potatoes and chickpeas of a Paris couscous, but good green peppers and yellow squash piled high, too, the chunk of gamy lamb topping it tender). There, the few guys in slacks and open-collared casual shirts eating are seated at the rows of tables so they are all facing the small TV hung high up, watching the news. The news includes some clips of U.S. soldiers in dun camouflage fatigues and with

automatic weapons ducking around the side streets of occupied Baghdad, looking confused, even outright scared; the
sniper attacks and bombings of this the summer of 2003 have
already begun. Tired from having gotten up not long past
dawn to make sure I was out at CDG in time for my flight
despite a near-total public-transit strike in Paris, I go back to
the hotel, stretch out still dressed on the made bed, and read
through the introduction to my Penguin Classics edition of
Salammbô; it is a commentary I haven't looked at yet, written
by the translator, the aforementioned A.J. Krailsheimer.

Tunis has a trolley system. Even this late at night, the
empty kelly-green trams with their buttery lit windows pass
slowly by in the empty street right below my window, rumbling, and the overhead electric connections flash blue light
in the darkness, which is nice. The stark modern room has
white walls, and it smells of sandalwood furniture polish for
the heavy dark-wood fare, an aroma that's somehow really
nice, too, spicy. I suppose I already wish I was going to have
more than two weeks in Tunisia—the place feels that right.

Also, I suppose I have no idea then that there's eventually
going to be a real bonus on this trip, and in a way it will grow
out of my preliminary brushes with sadness before coming to
Tunis; it will be one of those Big Realizations (keep both caps)
that don't come along very often, for boneheaded me, anyway.

Krailsheimer begins his introduction by flatly stating that
"nobody but Flaubert" could have written *Salammbô*, which
is true, of course, then he devotes the several following pages to basically defending, at the expense of celebrating, the
book. To be frank, that's often the tenor of even much of the
appreciative criticism I've seen on it, the curse it has been
saddled with in what passes for literary history.

5. *Salammbô* and Its Controversy

In 1857, right after his popular success with *Madame Bovary*—success helped no small amount by the novel being cause for a famous court trial charging obscenity and suggesting anticlericalism—Flaubert started making plans for a novel about ancient Carthage. By his own count, he had already read a hundred books on its almost mythical civilization.

He had long been fascinated with what for many Europeans at the time were the intriguing lands of the East, though work on the novel wasn't coming to life for him. Flaubert hit a hard wall when he realized that he had no chance of writing about a place he hadn't seen firsthand, even if he had considerable experience elsewhere in that part of the world from travel when younger. To borrow Steegmuller's translation of a letter from Flaubert to a friend:

> I absolutely must make a trip to Africa…. Once again I'll live on horseback and sleep in a tent…. But this trip will be a short one. I need to go only to El Kef (thirty leagues from Tunis), and explore the environs of Carthage within a radius of twenty leagues, in order to acquaint myself thoroughly with the landscapes I'll be describing…I'm a third of the way through the second chapter. The book will have fifteen. As you see, I've barely begun. Under the best circumstances, I'll not be finished for two years.

He was right on one count: the eventual product did contain fifteen chapters, but deciding after he went to Carthage that he previously had too much all wrong ("everything I have done on my novel has to be done over") and with the

Flaubertian obsession of elevating prose itself to something close to sacred, the creation of it a visionary, semi-religious experience (or, to put it another way, just saying "*le mot juste*" doesn't do justice to the full transcendent rhapsody of the process), *Salammbô* was five years—long and wearying—in the making. It was published in 1862, when he was forty-one.

The novel is based on a revolt of unpaid mercenaries in the Carthaginian army during the Punic Wars, when Carthage—originally founded by the Phoenicians who set out from the area of Syria/Lebanon—fought Rome for dominance of the Mediterranean. Often labeled the Mercenaries War (241-238 BC), the conflict, historians say, called into question the very premise of Carthage's military power, which had always combined a crack navy with well-paid mercenary soldiers, all skillful professionals, recruited from throughout the ancient world. It was this formula that did later allow Hannibal (247-183 BC) to set out by sea and then parade his fabled elephants—the equivalent of today's state-of-the-art combat tanks—across the snowy Alps and nearly bring Rome to heel, before Rome finally triumphed, invading and brutally conquering Carthage. The Romans burned the city to the ground in 146 BC; they built their own city on top of the charred ruins, sticking to the original name of Carthage (in Phoenician, "New City"), for what was to become the second most important metropolis in their own vast empire, before the Vandals invaded after that and then the Arabs from the East coming in after them. Against the backdrop of the revolt, Flaubert's novel centers on a star-crossed love between one of the triumvirate of leaders of the mercenary troops, a rugged yet sensitive young Numidian named Mâtho, who himself probably should have been a lyric poet and not any military commander, and Salammbô. She is the daughter of the top Carthaginian general, a ravishingly beautiful but hauntingly strange young woman; sometimes very cold in her ways, she was raised by priests of the Punic goddess Tanit. The novel's battle scenes are graphic, and there is also detailed depiction of the Punic practice of sacrifice of children to the gods. The novel's characterization is mostly a matter of voices speaking directly, often gushingly, from the heart in set speeches rather than in any realistic way, maybe as in an opera (Maupassant described *Salammbô* as exactly that in a published appreciation of the book, with Flaubert being his beloved mentor and a fellow Norman). What Krailsheimer poses—that nobody but Flaubert could have written it—is largely due to the characteristic richly handsome prose, pure Flaubertian. However, on just about every other count the book has been considered a questionable offering, even seen as "un-Flaubertian" (odder than his apprentice-work novel *La Tentation de Saint Antoine*, with one article I read bluntly labeling *Salammbô* as "Flaubert's mistake"), and the situation has been that way ever since F. first read chapters of it in manuscript to literary friends, including the Goncourt brothers; apparently, they tried to gently convince Flaubert (this is just what a writer needs from buddies when you show them something you wrote that you're personally crazy about) that he would be wise to put it in the drawer and not pursue its publication.

But it was published. And it did sell well—as said, *Madame Bovary* had already established Flaubert's name in the marketplace—though most critics at first bombed it for alleged historical inaccuracies. The tastemaker of the day Sainte-Beuve attacked it in no less than a lengthy, three-installment essay;

an admirer of Sainte-Beuve, Flaubert labored to answer the criticism in a series of long and defensive letters of his own. Sainte-Beuve even questioned the essential subject, wanted to know "Why Carthage?"—a civilization that had left few traces and whose everyday customs and lifestyle were virtually unknown, a comparatively blank ledger to the modern world; if ancient history were to be examined, Sainte-Beuve argued, wouldn't glorious Greece or glorious Rome have been a better choice? Further, Sainte-Beuve asked why write of what he saw as a footnote even in Carthage's history, the incident of a mercenary revolt, therefore making the novel's subject still more marginal?

And the criticism segued right into the twentieth century, with Marxist critic Georg Luckács seeing it as mere bourgeois indulgence in pretty words and romantic clichés fit for the tastes of "shop girls." And then the late Edward Said entering the discussion in his book-length 1979 study *Orientalism*. He holds up *Salammbô* as contributing to the tendency—which he argues got full venting in the nineteenth century—of Europeans viewing the Orient as a territory of The Other (the "Orient" at the time was often considered the Middle East and Islamic environs), a place savagely irrational, sorely in need of colonizing Europeans' organization and moral refinement. Such a perception of the region, Said emphasizes, remains strong today and has become a tool for Western political power and hegemony (the latter, like "gaze," recently another one of those "in" words for scholars, I guess); he says it fuels more of the condescending ethnocentric stereotyping by the West of people living in that part of the globe, specifically the Muslim inhabitants, as very inferior, an outlook tracing clear back to the Crusades.

Which *does* make sense. And did you notice how in the build-up to the Iraq War, Saddam Hussein was continually shown in evening TV news reports with stock footage of him wearing an oversize gangster's fedora and brandishing an automatic rifle on the dais, or unsheathing and wildly waving around a huge ceremonial saber? And, you know, I always greatly admired Edward Said, and I would say that my own politics remain close to his; plus, reading him, I certainly always appreciate his graceful and balanced critical prose itself. But his fundamental thesis in *Orientalism* veers toward the simplistic, and when I came upon what he says about *Salammbô* before making this trip, I got the feeling that as fair as he tries to be in treating Flaubert (who doesn't get raked over the glowing accusatory coals to the same degree as a noisy Christian traveler like Chateaubriand, also some lesser-known early journalists he criticizes; Flaubert and the very dreamy—and oh-so-eerie—Gérard de Nerval are given gentler critical treatment by Said when he addresses their writing about the so-called Orient), yes, as fair as he attempts to be with Flaubert, Said—not to put too fine a point on it—is wrong in even implying that one might take this sort of critical approach concerning *Salammbô*.

Or possibly, as with so much political literary criticism lately that repeatedly assaults "canonized" literature, Said just "doesn't get it." And while considering myself pretty much as respectfully PC in everyday life as the next person, I also know when to abandon the simple, though often admirably idealistic, logic of that tack. I know that when it comes to Art, the ground rules change, have nothing whatsoever to do with political agenda, really. And most anybody who has written creative fare himself or herself and therefore experienced the singular feeling of hitting on something uncannily transcendent when you are sitting before the glowing computer screen, let's say, pecking away at the black keyboard of your overpriced Mac PowerBook G4, let's also say, he or she *definitely* knows that to be the case. Indeed, it means to actually produce on the page, while writing, a fine turn of phrase in a line of poetry or a smooth meshing of events for a twist of drama in a novel that goes *beyond* reason, as you sense the icy, satisfyingly clear transport of the metaphysical and the whispering of the larger wonder of the world, which you hope you can let a reader—rich or poor, established or disenfranchised—savor for a minute or two, if only to know the full capacity of one's imagination and the extraordinary human beings we *all* are (kind of a William James moment, a variety of religious experience, no doubt, for both the writer and eventually the reader). Up against the strong effect of such artistic magic, argument via practical deductive reasoning and whatever else helps to render so many matters for literary scholars lately PC or not PC sours like coffee cream left in the faculty-lounge refrigerator too long, with, worse, most of the opaque high-tech linguistic "theory" that has earned many a party promotion and tenure in literature (perpetrated by talents surely less gifted than socially concerned, elegantly expressive Said) itself taking on the look of but the diversion of a bunch of giggly adolescents goofing around in the local video arcade.

Which again means that it often seems there's little *important*—to employ that earlier adjective—coming from those academics, but there is—to try to salvage a point made in the midst of the gusting wind of the last paragraph—much *important* coming from a book like *Salammbô*.

Which could be the real and more significant controversy about the novel—argument on just how it does, in fact, manage to wield such inexplicable power.

6. Hey, Here's an Idea

I won't go as far as Saul Bellow once did in proposing the abolishment of all departments at colleges and universities devoted to study of modern literature. Bellow said that a better tack might be to just let people *read* the books on their own, remove the meddling middleman who has been undermining the original reader-author love affair altogether too much lately. But here's what I do say: What if every literature professor were forced to try his or her hand at attempting to write a few short stories or a sheaf of poems?

I mean, there was a time when a lot of scholars had tried this somewhere along the way—future lit profs once wide-eyed undergrads often daydreaming of becoming writers themselves, yet eventually putting that aside and dedicatedly going on to lecture and write about literature—a time when professors unabashedly *loved* the books they taught and when they understood the specialness of them better, possibly because they had tried some writing themselves. I suppose that today most undergrads with any creative inclination usually go into the many graduate M.F.A. programs currently available, and, I hate to say it, those who aspire to be academics simply proceed directly to a Ph.D. program, without much artistic sidetracking, for what is a practical, very divergent route and with a completely different relationship to the literature they should be in awe of. (I remember once seeing a young literature professor at my own university coming out of the chairman's office; the chairman had just given her the good news that her promotion with tenure was approved by the university, and she was announcing gleefully and flauntingly—also add some nerdy nasal intonation—to anybody she ran into plodding along the green linoleum of the department's building: "I'll never have to read a primary text again!") You know, attempting to produce some fiction or poetry, the scholar might experience a measure of what I have been talking about, learn firsthand the essence of the unique creative rush if only in a stolen glimpse of it, and, with that happening, suddenly Art and aesthetics might be in vogue again in English departments. Years ago Harold Bloom, an indisputably major modern-day scholar and critic, wrote an awful novel that came my way for review, a virtually unreadable performance, but I've often thought that the fact he *attempted* to produce literature himself gave the man something extra, an insight, that maybe has afforded him the decidedly rare edge he has—as lovably cranky as he can be—over so many more predictable contemporary literary observers.

I know, I'm *really* wandering, but it all will eventually figure in. Because I am thinking about this kind of stuff during my time in Tunisia, as I think more and more about the story of Flaubert and *Salammbô*. Despite the amount of controversy, the novel did emerge somewhat triumphant, principally in France. It became for many a revered Secret Text, you might say; the lush diction and visionary power of it, even the psychological complexity of its doomed central love affair, definitely and revealingly Sadeian in a way, had a great influence on the French Parnassians and Symbolists. In their own defining contrariness, they went against the grain, adopted it as a manifesto. Painters also took it to heart, the nineteenth-century Symbolist master Gustave Moreau most prominent among them. Actually, on this current *Salammbô* mission, I'd made it a point while in Paris to seek out Moreau's spacious studio, which has long been maintained as a museum for his work. It's up in the staidly gray Seventeenth Arrondissement and chock full of his billboard-sized visions of classical and Biblical scenes in wild, ultra-radiant color that go beyond the simple hallucinatory, almost qualifying as bona fide psychedelic. Gustave Moreau—now there was one guy who obviously did "get it."

7. Plasticize Your Documents

I'm at the top of the wide main boulevard, Avenue Bourguiba, at twilight.

This is right before the ancient gateway arch built by the first Arabs here, which announces the entry to the old city and the Medina (near this very arch, supposedly, Cervantes once fought the "infidel"). I notice on the sidewalk a tiny key-making kiosk with an old, rather Jules Verne-ish red-metal contraption outside, coin-operated, in which you can laminate identity cards or the like. A sign says in French that your documents are important, their good condition, and you should protect them, plasticize them. I know that in a country like this such carried documents *are* very important, the police regularly asking to see one's papers, yet it also strikes me right then and there as almost a metaphor for what Flaubert was trying to do with his constant mad note-taking while in Tunisia that he writes of in his letters—Flaubert attempting to preserve everything, beat time, so he could preserve it even better than that, really plasticize it, when he eventually did sit down for the five long years of surely *mot juste*-ing in rainy Normandy. I ask myself if all art isn't just that, what the sign advertises:

PLASTIFICATION POUR VOS DOCUMENTS

That evening, as every evening, I again stroll up and down Avenue Bourguiba, the outdoor cafés packed, the broad sidewalks crowded with other strolling folk, a repeated, nightly celebration as thousands of starlings chirpingly swoop in dramatic dark clouds against the genuinely lavender twilight sky.

8. Good Twenty-Five-Buck Reeboks

I keep thinking an awful lot about Flaubert and *Salammbô*. True to Flaubert's model, I'm also up to my own habit of taking notes madly, stopping in the middle of a downtown sidewalk or in the Medina to do so, CIA style, maybe. This thinking about *Salammbô* and Flaubert himself in Tunisia has given me an organizing focus for the trip, but I'm also jotting down ideas for short stories of my own to be set in Tunisia, writing the invisible narratives in my head—plot outlines, transition sentences—as I meander around on my new and bouncy twenty-five-buck Reebok track shoes, black and white, and take in everything (wow, look at that side-street café with the long row of men sitting out front in red *chechia* caps puffing their ornate hookahs, a perfect picture! wow, look at that massive old Art Deco Jewish synagogue on Avenue de la Liberté, like an armed enclave with the dozen or so soldiers toting AK-47s at the front gate, a painful sign of the times), and meander around some more.

I go back to the couscous place just about every evening, sticking with a winner.

I'm saving my own assault on the ruins of Carthage till later, preparing for it. At the hotel I reread the letters I photostatted that Flaubert posted from his own trip (to repeat, there aren't many, unlike the piles of them from the longer journey to Middle Eastern countries when younger, and he was only at the ruins of Carthage for several days), and I'm going through the complete text of Salammbô again, remembering that I forgot to pick up a copy in French in Paris and hoping I can find one here. I want to have everything fresh in my mind, my cerebral guidebook, in order to see it all through maybe F.'s own—how should I put this—"gaze"? As for the Saint Augustine I packed, I find myself skimming it, the sections on his time in Carthage turning out to be comparatively brief. And while I do again look once or twice to see the signature of my sister's college roommate on the title page, it's tough to get into the prose's often bombastic preaching, what I vaguely remember from when I myself had to read it (or at least pretend I did) at a Catholic boys' school as a kid. But I can say that when I think now of Saint Augustine's frequently quoted line once more about how the world is a book and a person who has not traveled has read only a page of that book, such a thought understandably resonates for me at the moment.

I've already relocated to another hotel called the Majestic, a white Art Nouveau wedding-cake rise from the time of the French Protectorate (the admittedly hegemonistically named "Protectorate" did certainly happen, 1881-1956); the Majestic might be a little shabby, but I like how my airy, spacious room has a balcony overlooking the busy Avenue de Paris.

The place is much better than the Hôtel Omrane, where I suffered a bad spider bite that has left a sizable strawberry rash on my leg. I'm finding Tunis more and more attractive almost by the hour. I take especially long walks through the maze of the old city, the Medina, which has been kept intact with designation as a UNESCO World Heritage landmark, visiting the mosques and the palaces and the ornate mausoleums of the old Arab and Ottoman rulers there, and everybody is thoroughly friendly. A smiling young cop stops me to ask in French how I am enjoying the city, proudly telling me how many languages he speaks. The athletically handsome manager in a good suit at the Hôtel Majestic turns out to be a former soccer star for the locally revered Club Africain team, and, a soccer fan myself, I talk to him at length about the sport, fancying, maybe, it's the manly way Hemingway used to talk to hotel managers about sport—or about bullfighting, anyway, in the persona of the Jake character in *The Sun Also Rises*. Any problem stemming from my being in a Muslim country in the time of the major U.S. mess-up in Iraq is softened by saying to people right off the bat in my French, *"Je suis américain, malheureusement,"* which usually elicits a smile, then maybe some honest dialogue about the current situation. If that doesn't work, I bring up Jack Kennedy, who remains honored in the country because he and Jackie were good friends of the founder of modern-day independent Tunisia, the progressive Habib Bourguiba—the Kennedy reference seems capable of breaking the ice if anybody seems more critical of my nationality. A last, trumping resort if I want to indisputably assert my personal credibility as an American is simply to declare, emphatically: *"Bush, il est fou, c'est un idiot!"*

9. "Miami, That's My Kind of City!"

One afternoon I'm strolling beside some impressive futuristic government buildings at the edge of the downtown, and when I stop to write down a few notes, a guy about thirty comes up to me. He introduces himself, saying he suspected I was American. He's an overweight, wide-grinning sort wearing what looks like frat-boy attire, complete with a neat yellow polo shirt and good dress slacks; I figure he works in one of the government offices. He has no interest in getting into any Bush-bashing, and he tells me cheerily in French that his dream has always been to go not simply to America but specifically to Miami.

To quote him: "Miami, that's my kind of city!"

He talks more about Miami. After ten minutes of conversation, I conclude that for him it's ultra-exotic, with the beach and the girls in Miami (actually, both of which he could find nearby on the Tunisian coast, where the tourist industry is garishly developed); probably the romantic aura of the big-time crime in Miami as celebrated in TV shows and movies contributes to an adventurous image, too, the fast life—in other words, for him its draw is the Otherness of the savage and morally deficient West, and even if the paradigm doesn't entail much hegemony, it's rather a reverse Orientalism, no?

Innocent enough.

10. Ancient Carthage, the First Assault

As for the ruins of ancient Carthage being a tourist attraction, those ruins do suffer from their own longtime bad rap, I realize. The truth of the matter is that there isn't much left, and whatever was Punic that has been excavated is overshadowed by the excavations more extensive and dramatic for the Roman city later there. Most sources warn it takes some time to appreciate the scant vestiges of the Punic era that exist today, even get a bead on what remains.

Carthage is now a suburb north of Tunis, where the city's modern airport is located, in fact. While both the Punic and Roman leaders believed in its prime strategic location overlooking the Gulf of Tunis—a wide inlet of the luminescently azure Mediterranean tucked in on either side by jagged purple mountains rising to make for long peninsulas across the way—the Arabs when they came established their city at a lesser settlement that eventually became Tunis, farther inland and set off from full proximity to the sea by Lake Tunis. On a hot weekday midmorning, I take the relatively empty little commuter train that goes to the northern suburbs, posh white villas abundant once you get beyond the industrial hodgepodge of Tunis's port area. Many of the stations along the seaside route have names with Punic ties that could almost be an index for Flaubert's novel: one is "Salammbô"; another "Hannibal," Salammbô's baby brother, who makes a relatively brief guest appearance in the book; another "Hamilcar," her father and the fearsome Carthaginian top general. I step off the train at the empty Hannibal station—very neatly suburban and built by the colonizers with, indeed, considerable Oriental whimsy, a blue-and-white cottage-style affair of onion arches and embellishing arabesques, cascading bougainvillea everywhere. I start walking in the opposite direction of the sea, up a long, steep road blanketed with fallen tree petals—strikingly bright orange—passing a swank tennis club and more villas, heading toward the epicenter of the several scattered "Archeological Sites," Byrsa Hill. It's hot, will be closing in on a hundred before the day is done, and this first assault on what is the main site in the ruins of Carthage is pretty unfocused for me, even disorienting.

The summit, where the Punic temple stood and a location prominent in *Salammbô*, was later built over with a Roman temple. Then the French constructed a massive and gaudily yellow basilica, still standing, in honor of Saint Louis, a.k.a. Louis IX; having set out on a Crusade launched from the south of France, he succumbed to a typhoid epidemic and died here in 1270. The 360 degrees of vistas is nearly too much—the sea, the mountains, even distantly white Tunis with its few industrial smokestacks in the panorama—and to make everything more disorienting, there is the heat. Though I gunked up with coconut-fragrant sun block and am wearing khakis and a long-sleeve shirt to ward off the rays, I forgot my Red Sox baseball cap, plus this day I didn't even pack a plastic bag with the mandatory liter bottle of water that half the Tunisian citizenry seem to tote around at all times. A long esplanade in front of a white museum, which was formerly the monastery for the giant basilica that itself is now a gallery and performance arts center, makes you feel like you've just stepped into a de Chirico canvas, the way they've set upright some truncated Roman columns and broken statuary; the heaps of brown stone ruins directly below the overlook constitute the excavated Punic Quarter, claimed to be the remnants of a neighborhood from the old civilization, but for me right now they look like not much more than, yes, heaps of brown stones, a lot of weeds and even plenty of trash interspersed. I have equally little luck in responding when I wander into the museum that of- fers both Roman and Punic artifacts, and not helping the situation within, there is the presence of several of the kind of for-hire guides who prey on naïve tourists, one guy now spieling away in bad, obnoxiously loud English that can be heard throughout the rooms to two British women, fragile and quite old. I tell myself they are *such* easy marks that no self-respecting, hustling tour guide should even attempt to hit on them, and this guy should be absolutely ashamed of himself (the standard M.O. appears to be to approach foreigners as a helpful friend and tag along with gladly given information—and then, when the spieling is done, demand some exorbitant fee for the unrequested services). To be frank, *none* of it is coming together today, either the lay of what was once the Carthaginian city or any sense of Flaubert bouncing around on a mule (not a horse, as he predicted in his letter) and doing his research out here. To be really frank, I am lost in a moment of wondering what the *hell* I am even doing on this trip, dodging some personal obligations back home and abandoning my writing for a few weeks; I know I've always used travel as a way to escape responsibility. Having skipped lunch, I'm a bit dizzy, and add to that, I'm sunburned already, despite the lotion.

I make the half-hour trek in the pulsating heat back to the station, take the train a little farther north to the resort village of Sidi Bou Said on a high, cliffed point of land. It's a ridiculously beautiful place of a seemingly enforced color code on the villas, with white for the stucco walls and blue for the decorative tiles and shutters; there's a nest of winding cobbled streets at the top of the Gibraltar-like rise of it, a yacht harbor below. It's sometimes called the Saint-Tropez of North Africa, exclusive, immaculate, with many signs saying where you can't park, where you can't walk. The guidebooks note how it has been a favorite haunt of every French cultural celebrity spending time in Tunisia from Paul Klee to Michel Foucault to Simone de Beauvoir, as well as Frédéric Mitterrand, the controversial French actor and producer (nephew of the former Monsieur le Président himself), who seems to have been a longtime resident, and I do remember that I saw an expensive coffee-table photo book in a bookstore in Tunis for which he provides the chatty introduction: *Les Maisons de Sidi Bou Said*. Beautiful as it is, Sidi Bou Said doesn't look very attractive to me in my present mood, the profusion here of stupid and indulgent wealth, haughtily oblivious of, even walling itself off from, any discomfort—or any *reality*—in the world elsewhere.

And trudging around Sidi Bou Said I remember—to make matters even worse—a scene of a badly lame little kid of ten or so. Barefoot, he was dressed in ragged white and trying to sell sprigs of jasmine to those sitting at the outdoor cafés on Avenue Bourguiba the evening before; in Tunisia, men will buy fragrant jasmine—the national flower—to put behind the ear, a ubiquitous local tradition. The kid was having no luck selling, and he seemed to give up at one point, or to just forget about it, and looking at his flower holder (the boys who sell them stick the stems of the white-petaled jasmine into a wooden ball, which becomes almost a big star in the hand), he held it up as if he were indeed but a carefree kid with a fireworks sparkler, ran limpingly in meaningless circles, smiling and gazing up at that star he waved, maybe at all the brighter stars of the indigo Tunisian night sky above, too, the kid contentedly playing, even singing to himself. Yes, for a minute, anyway, he was merely a *happy kid* and not somebody shackled to a life in the street and a physical disability that will make that life so hard for him, as in his innocence he didn't know such consequences and all of that yet. To witness it broke my heart, and I think of it now in Sidi Bou Said—how absurd a world it is that juxtaposes that kind of ill fortune beside the smug opulence of a place such as Sidi Bou Said, with its gleaming BMWs and its handsome walled-in villas and its chic, beautiful-people inhabitants easing around behind oversize protecting sunglasses. I think of my own sadness I indulged in (the sense of loss I get whenever I go back to my summer place, often there alone and with only the remembering of happier times to surround me), and I feel more than stupid for such self-centered indulgence, suspect that possibly social concern has to figure into *everything*, and art and literature can be but indulgence as well. I take the train back to Tunis, worn out from a day that didn't add up to much whatsoever, other than doubt.

And I concede what you have to sometimes concede: Not every day of travel, just as not every night of dreaming, takes you to where you really want to go. At the Hôtel Majestic I spend a couple of subdued days rereading yet another time the passages of *Salammbô* that describe the vanished ancient city of Carthage, still trying to get some valid orientation. I also go through, once more, the photostatted Flaubert letters for clues that might help me conjure up a better sense of his own visit there.

My second assault on ancient Carthage will prove the beginning of my breakthrough, the already alluded to Big Realization. (*Salammbô* uses potboiling, cliff-hanging tricks throughout, especially at the end of chapters, so if I do appear to be trying quite hard with the narrative teasing, at least I'm in respected company). Listen a little more.

11. Ancient Carthage, the Second Assault

Those good Reeboks cushiony below me, the dark blue baseball cap with a big red *B* on it firmly on my head, a liter bottle of mineral water along with my guidebooks and maps packed in a flimsy plastic supermarket sack, I return to the downtown station and board the teapot-whistling little commuter train to head up the coast again. I soon realize it's a mistake to travel on Sunday, the cars crowded with a large chunk of Tunis's population escaping the city for the many good beaches far less exclusive than the one at Sidi Bou Said, and standing up I'm soaked in sweat; but when two teenage guys jimmy the locked latch mechanism and open the doors once we get rolling, the breeze on the causeway that crosses over the huge steamy puddle of Lake Tunis is wonderful. I remember Flaubert, both in a letter and in the novel, talking of flocks of pink flamingoes alighting from the lake, and while I haven't witnessed the phenomenon personally, I can easily *envision* it as the train rattles along—which is exactly what I do. And already I somehow sense it's going to be a better day, a banner one, in fact.

Stepping off at the Salammbô station this time, I plan to make the entire loop of the so-called Archeological Sites, a half-dozen spots separated by a half mile or so of walking in between them. It's still as hot as it was a couple of days before, but I'm much better prepared now. I will scribble notes for the next four or five hours, walking, scribbling, and walking some more.

** The Tophet, or ancient burial plot, is a fenced-in, unkempt patch amid more white villas close to the sea. It offers several unearthed crypts and hundreds of strewn-about *stèles*, more or less small obelisk headstones bearing the mark

87

of the goddess Tanit, Salammbô's personal deity, which consists of a pyramid topped with a cross bar and a ring, the symbols of the sun and moon above that.

Flaubert figures in largely on this. And even if the site wasn't excavated when he was here in 1858, he did get to know the Belgian archeologists studying Carthage at the time. The Peruvian novelist Mario Vargas Llosa in his book on *Madame Bovary*, a masterful meditation titled *The Perpetual Orgy*, talks of visiting the small Flaubert museum in Croisset and seeing such a *stèle*, which apparently F. had lugged back with him to France. Right from the start, a charge against *Salammbô* was that it indulged in gratuitous violence, not only the battles but particularly the episode when the war with the rebelling mercenaries isn't going too well for the Carthaginians and they sacrifice some of their children to the god Moloch in hopes of reversing their luck; such rumored child sacrifice wasn't documented when Flaubert wrote of it, though remains found at this very site later confirmed it. To be honest, the violence and graphic descriptions of the killing in the novel are fully nightmarish, à la Cormac McCarthy in *Blood Meridian*, and somebody adhering to the critical approach of Edward Said, in the spirit of *Orientalism,* might say that Flaubert indulged in literary sensationalism at the expense of a true depiction of the Carthaginians, Flaubert allegedly perpetuating the image of Oriental savagery. But the scenes are also handsomely written, effective. Further, Flaubert might have been noticeably condescending in some of his letters about what he observed during his extensive Eastern travels (such as in describing his trip to Constantinople), yet in carefully reading *Salammbô*, one soon learns that the Carthaginians, master merchants, are by and large shown as highly refined in their government and commerce, while the few times Gauls—Europeans—are mentioned (there are some among the recruited mercenaries) they seem to be portrayed as markedly *uncivilized*, seen as drunken louts.

At the Tophet, in the building heat, a wiry mustached guy has been tagging after me, the only customer there, wanting to be my guide. I politely tell him in French I don't need one, and I know that here I want to experience the place on my own, think about it without any intrusion, which I do. When I leave, he is sitting on a folding chair outside the gatehouse sulking, most likely because he didn't get my business. I offer a friendly smile and explain that I didn't need him because I already have a guide—I hold up the Rough Guides guidebook, its clichéd photo of a desert oasis on the emerald-green cover—and he shakes his head, waving it away as if it's an annoying fly. He tells me the book is no good, and it doesn't have the real story.

"*Les enfants*," he says gruffly.

Sitting there, he makes a chopping motion at the back of his neck, winces in put-on agony, pantomiming what happened to the children.

"*Les enfants*," he repeats it, emphasizing, "*vous n'avez pas la verité, monsieur.*" I don't have the truth.

Either he hasn't read *Orientalism* and therefore isn't suitably PC, or like Flaubert, possibly, he knows what sells. In any case, at the Tophet, Punic Carthage is beginning to emerge for me, in sort of a "know my religion, know my civilization" way.

** I walk past still more white villas on a suburban road along the sea, and soon find the Punic Ports, an important aspect of the ancient city of Carthage proper. Today these

are but two connected brackish suburban ponds, one vaguely rectangular and one vaguely circular with a small island
studding its center, yet the geometry of them was once exact.
And at one time this was all a prime symbol of Carthaginian
dominance, the outer port for merchant vessels and the inner
one for a large fleet of naval vessels, which docked like neat
spokes around that central, and formerly perfect, sphere of
the island. On the island was built a nautical roundhouse
to service the long, graceful ships, which were powered by
both wind and rowing galley slaves in their venturing to
the many outposts of the empire as far off as Cartagena in
Spain (the name deriving from "Carthage") and clear to
West Africa's Atlantic coastline. The Euclidean precision of
the whole layout is definitely no longer intact, and there are
just the undulating grassy banks and surrounding grounds
landscaped like a park, with sun-hungry golden tamarisk and
giant ornamental oleander, vivid scarlet; a number of well-
heeled residents from the neighborhood are out for morning
dog-walking or some casual fishing in the ponds. However,
what was for me only a model or a drawing before—all the
guidebook illustrations of the original city stress the classic
pattern of these Punic Ports at the foot of Byrsa Hill, the
once-exact geometry of them—now becomes more clear,
easy to picture, and it takes being here, this close to the tepid
water, to start to truly understand the layout. I can also picture the fine vessel of General Hamilcar, the princess's father
in *Salammbô,* gliding through the gates of the ports (they
were both entirely within the city's protecting walls then),
returned at last from the Roman campaign to eventually attempt to rescue his people from the mercenary uprising, as
happens in the novel. So for me here, it's a matter of "know

my ports, know my civilization," and I'm beginning to get a solid feel for the larger plan of the city, the geography described in *Salammbô*. An interesting note is that it was Chateaubriand, one of Said's named offenders, who in 1805 deduced that these unimposing ponds, neglected for centuries, were actually the famous ports of the city alluded to in ancient texts, something nobody else had quite figured out before.

I've been at it for about two hours already, but with the baseball cap and the water bottle, even a roll of crackers and a banana packed for sustenance, I don't notice the time pass.

** Farther on, right beside the sea, is a plot called the Magon Quarter, or the German Excavations, unearthed by, naturally, German archeologists. This site offers low foundations of what might have been a Punic city block, weedy; nevertheless, in true German tradition (they were zealous archeologists) it's much more organized than most of the other ruins, outfitted with illustrated placards explaining everything in French, Arabic, *and* German (which looks weird, because for me Tunisia itself feels anything *but* German). After that are the Roman Baths, a large site with substantial remnants of the buildings—stone pillars and interior arches—beside the sea, which reminds you that most of the Carthaginian ruins *are* Roman and not Punic, ditto regarding the site of the Roman Houses, up toward Byrsa Hill, also the nearby Roman Amphitheatre there, which has been completely reconstructed as a venue for music concerts and the like; the profusion of Roman ruins perhaps also emphasizes exactly how *gone and vanished* any idea of the Punic itself really is. Hot, sweating, I look at my watch to see it's early afternoon now, two or so.

And as I plod back up that same sloping asphalt pavement strewn with orange-colored petals to Byrsa Hill that I walked before, now in the fully hundred-degree afternoon heat under a sky flawlessly deep blue, I am tired, and the swelling on my leg left from the spider bite is increasingly aggravated by the heat and my khakis rubbing against it. But I do have some sense at long last of not only the layout of the original city but also how Flaubert must have felt out here, putting the puzzle together for himself. Flaubert visited Carthage before many of the major Punic archeological discoveries, as said; he was chastised at first by the supposed experts in France for allegedly having gotten wrong in his novel many of the details about the physical trappings of the Punic city, though later he was proven to be remarkably accurate on that score—uncannily so, according to some sources.

    ** And atop Byrsa Hill again, deserted of tourists who are probably all at the cooling beaches now, I look out from that same high esplanade in front of the yellow façade of the Saint Louis Basilica and the white monastery beside it that is now the artifact museum, and everything here suddenly comes alive and makes sense, too.

    The prime vista is now for me *exactly* the way Flaubert described it in the novel, up here where the temple was, running down the hill past the ruins of the excavated Punic Quarter, where you *can* discern the outline of streets and houses, then stretching—after more posh villas and clusters of fruit trees and wiggly cypresses, far below—to the Punic Ports, which were previously only nondescript ponds indeed the last time I was here, but now exist in their full significance; beyond lies the sparkling Gulf of Tunis, framed on either side by the aforementioned purple mountains and opening out to the wide, wide Mediterranean Sea, once near entirely ruled by the mighty Carthaginians who on this very spot could boast of offering the greatest civilization of their era.

But now all of that is absolutely gone, like everything else will be gone, including me, my summer house that deals me considerable sadness lately, even the kid selling flowers (the poor little guy) there on Avenue Bourguiba beneath the aching stars a few nights before; the power of the ruins of Punic Carthage is not so much in what remains, scant compared to that of other excavated sites of former civilizations worldwide, but in how much has vanished, left only to the imagination—but the imagination is supremely powerful. And I like to think of Flaubert out here thinking exactly the same thing, and, not to be presumptuous, I sense more than ever what it must have been like for him perhaps thinking the same thing, imagining it all, planning his book.

I wander through the empty rooms of the museum again, no guides hustling tourists in this heat. I write some notes concerning the holdings in the showcases of fine Punic jewelry (pink coral; blue scarab; exquisite cast gold), which could have been similar to Salammbô's celebrated rich adornment, and then I linger in front of the museum's maps and reconstructed models of the city, studying them. Several hours on my feet, I'm very tired now, but comfortably so. I feel I have found what I wanted and have experienced a breakthrough (but it will not turn out to be quite that way—*yet*) as I head back down the steep road, going toward the station at Hannibal.

Which is when I see a slim young woman, pretty, walking directly towards me, approaching me.

12. The Young German Woman Walks Away with the Ghost of Me

"*Bonjour,*" she says.

"*Bonjour,*" I say.

Sweating from the hike up the hill so that ribbons of her mahogany hair are glued to her forehead, her eyes pale, smiling though obviously weary herself, the young woman asks me in French if there are, generically, "any sites" around here. She is lost, it seems, without a map and just off the train at the Hannibal stop herself. Probably in her late twenties, there's something of the grad student about her, wearing functional beige pedal-pushers and a rumpled bland-plaid sleeveless blouse, what looks like very typical grad-student attire. In fact, she admits she is *totally* lost. We sit for a while on a bench at a bus stop in the deserted, stilled Sunday afternoon, laughing, my confessing how I was beyond totally lost myself on my first trip out here to Carthage. She explains she is staying with friends in Bizerte, a resort on the coast and formerly the Old World city of Hippo Diarrhytus (it predates even Carthage), and when I tell her I am American and try to make a joke about how Americans are currently not too popular in France, considering the international fiasco in Iraq, she tells me she is German and not French, saying, with a smile, that Americans are not very popular in Germany right now either. (My own French isn't good enough to pick up accents—I'm usually satisfied simply to hear myself functioning in the other language). I ask her where she's from and she says Frankfurt. She asks me why I'm in Tunis, and I go on with some energetic mush in French about Flaubert and *Salammbô*, which—surprisingly—appears to interest her;

she admits to having heard of the novel but not having read it, says that she now wishes she had read it before she came, if it is actually about Carthage, as I say. Even though I tell her that Byrsa Hill is the main attraction in this vicinity, the principal "site," she doesn't appear to want to pursue climbing up the steep hill any farther, saying, *"Peut-être un autre jour."* And when I tell her there is a winding side street, down the incline a ways and at the tennis club there, and that it leads over to the Roman Houses and the Roman Amphitheatre, she decides she will settle for those attractions today. It seems, however, that she just wants to go in the same direction as me. Well, I'm sane enough to know that, lost, she only wants company, and with regard to somebody my age, for her there's clearly no interest other than that—no, I'm not a young guy anymore, needless to add—but I do get the feeling she would tag along with me on the avuncular count alone if I were to encourage it, her continuing to hang on just about anything I say in my French, repeatedly laughing in her subdued, grad-student way. Together we descend the hill for a while, then part at the tennis club, going our separate ways. Off to find the other sites I recommended, she stops after a few steps and turns around to offer me a big final wave, as she stands there in the swallowing shade of the winding side street.

"Au revoir," she says again.

"Au revoir, et aussi bonne chance," I say, adding, *"Bonne chance, pour les sites."*

She smiles again, a pretty young woman soon walking away on a carpet of those fallen, bright-orange petals.

And I can't help but think of how when I was young and traveling on my own a good deal, I might sometimes meet a

girl in a youth hostel or just sightseeing and soon be spending time with her. (Why, I once fell head over heels, all but
thought I wanted to marry on the spot, a pudgy, gigglingly
bucktoothed, whitely blond Swiss girl, a lot of fun, who was
twenty-two years old and a secretary at a police station in
Geneva, which qualified her as an auxiliary cop herself; I
was a kid myself back then, and I met her on the Chihuahua
al Pacífico train that crosses the dramatic scenery of the high
mountains of northern Mexico when she was backpacking in
a yearlong grand trip around Latin America that she'd saved
up for, the pair of us happily traveling together for a few days,
ending up in a seedy, and perfect, little seaside fishing town
called Topolobampo across from the Baja Peninsula.) I think
of how things have certainly changed since then, but there's
no regret to any of it. Nevertheless, possibly contemplating
the ruins on Byrsa Hill has skewed time some for me. To
the point that I somehow seem to now see myself young and
dark-haired, somehow straighter and taller, too, a ghost of
me walking away with that young German woman, the two
of us laughing and together waving goodbye to the older guy
that *is* me in the Red Sox cap, standing there by himself and
holding a plastic bag with a water bottle and Rough Guides
guidebook—because I *am* older, which is how it should be,
of course, granting that the whole elusive concept of time
itself can often turn very spookily tricky.

When the train back to the city stops briefly at La Goulette-Vieille, the car only half full with people now quietly
returning from their day at the beach, I do catch a peek,
the slightest view, down the main street and to the sea. It is
where the aunt of my friend the Parisian professor, Claude
Lévy, once had the summer house he enjoyed so much as a

child, an area now funky and half industrialized, abutting Tunis's ever-expanding shipping port. I know that I am too beat to keep my promise to revisit the place for him. But what if I simply lie to him back in Paris, fabricate like Marlow does at the end in *Heart of Darkness?* What if I say that I went there, that even with the house gone, the place was beautiful (the white sand as soft as flour, the shaggy-headed palms rattling like castanets in the soft breeze, the Gulf of Tunis bluer than blue at this late hour of a summer Sunday winding down), to reinforce the image of it preserved in his own memory—*because his own memory is free of the shackles of Time, and that's the way the cherished spot remains in his own personal reality?* I like that idea.

Man, the day has proved a great one, and I feel good. But the Big Realization is *still* to come.

Listen just a little more.

13. Almost

So, my Carthage research just about accomplished, I log some old-fashioned sightseeing.

I leave the Hôtel Majestic for a few days and travel by bouncing long-distance bus out toward the edge of the Sahara and the city of Kairouan. Founded in 670, it was once the administrative seat for a large portion of Muslim North Africa, a place still considered the fourth holiest in Islam, seeing that a compatriot of the Prophet is entombed there. The fine golden crenellated walls of its vast Medina, the way that everything on street signs and such is in wispy Arabic and not French here, the architectural phenomenon of its imposing Great Mosque—the whole package makes it easy to understand how the place did such a number on a young Paul Klee in 1914; Klee proclaimed that to see Kairouan was to behold *A Thousand and One Nights* in reality, and he said the experience moved him so much, was so powerful, that it made him decide to return to Germany and at last get serious with his own painting. In making a loop by bus back to Tunis, I spend time in Sousse, a large seaside city now developed as a major Mediterranean beach resort with a ton of package-tour business. As welcoming as the sun and surf are in Sousse, it isn't my kind of scene (too many new high-rise hotels; also, one of those white, rubber-tired imitation choo-choo trains for tourists slowly snaking along the Corniche; and, most annoying for me, two shaved-headed young British guys who look like soccer hooligans in my small hotel—loud, red like boiled crabs, the heavier of the pair always wearing with his swimsuit a black T-shirt that announces "FBI" in big white lettering on the back, and under that in smaller print: "Female Body Inspector"), until eventually I'm glad to be back in Tunis. There I'm greeted like a celebrity by the staff at the once-opulent Majestic, who address me heartily as "Monsieur LaSalle," not only the former soccer star of a manager pleased to see me again, but also the elderly bellboy in his frayed, epauletted red jacket and the cleaning ladies as well, all remembering my generous tipping, I guess.

I finally buy a copy of *Salammbô* in French at a bookstore on Avenue Bourguiba. It's a cheap edition published by the Paris company Maxi-Livres that prints up uncopyrighted classics in functional, sturdily bound paper editions, an operation like Dover Books in the U.S. I'm at that stage when you've done most everything you're supposed to do on a trip. (Yes, I have "tuned in" on Flaubert's time in Carthage and, in being here, savored the wonder of a book that admittedly

is—when all is said and done—still an oddity in his oeuvre, *Salammbô;* my brain is cooking with *plenty* of new ideas
for fiction set in Tunisia, plus the research I've accomplished
will eventually render the essay you're now reading.) Before
dinner one evening I sit out on my hotel room's balcony
above the Avenue de Paris. I enjoy a bottle of Virgen lemon
soda (the chief local brand) and a small bag of paprika po-
tato chips I bought at the Monoprix on Avenue Charles de
Gaulle (being in a Muslim country encourages a cut-down
on alcohol, so no late-afternoon tallboy of beer for me—I
wouldn't even know of a street shop where to buy one in
Tunis), and I start reading *Salammbô* in the French edition.
It has an orange spine and the cover reproduces a scene of
busy activity in a palace that seems much more Roman than
Punic (you can't expect everything to be accurate on a two-
buck production like this). The thumping, meandering Arab
pop plays from a kiosk selling music tapes below; the horns
of the yellow taxis yap at each other during the rush hour
now on Avenue de Paris, lined with its fine, purple-flower-
ing jacarandas; the workers in their European attire pour out
of the old office buildings, including the sizable one for Star
Assurances across the street. Actually, from the balcony I can
see over the big Star Assurances building, have a good view,
well beyond that, of the low clutter of many white domes
that *is* the Tunis skyline.

But none of that has anything to do with my life at the
moment.

14. My Life at the Moment (I Think)
No, my life at the moment has nothing to do with that. I
am in a whirlwind of words—strong nouns and rich adjec-

tives and breathing verbs; drugging metaphors and orchestral polysyllabic rhythms, too—and I have been blown from wherever I am on a balcony above Avenue de Paris clear to a raucous Punic feast being held in ancient Carthage's luxuriant palatial gardens, organized for the soon-to-revolt mercenaries who have been recruited from every far-flung corner of the ancient world, gathered now to be honored for their victories abroad. Until that is interrupted by a door at the adjoining palace opening on a high terrace above, and entering the gardens is a wraith of a heartbreakingly lovely young woman almost powered by the milky moonlight itself; she marches into the feast as followed by two lines of pale eunuch priests hauntingly chanting low a hymn to the deities of Carthage. The woman is Salammbô, General Hamilcar Barca's daughter, and her priests are also from that noble Barca family, all descended from (this gets wild) the original conger eel that hatched the mystic egg in which the goddess Tanit, moonlight-charged herself, had long lay hidden.

15. OK, Even If You Don't Understand a Goddamned Word of French, Read this Aloud Yourself Wherever You Are and Tell Me What Happens, Because Here Is the Scene in the Novel of Princess Salammbô Entering that Feast:

Sa chevelure, poudrée d'un sable violet, et réunie en forme de tour selon la mode des vierges chananéennes, la faisait paraître plus grande. Des tresses de perles attachées à ses tempes descendaient jusqu'aux coins de sa bouche, rose comme une grenade entr'ouverte. Il y avait sur sa poitrine un

assemblage de pierres lumineuses, imitant par leur bigarru-
re les écailles d'un murène. Ses bras, garnis de diamants,
sortaient nus de sa tunique sans manches, étoilée de fleurs
rouges sur un fond tout noir. Elle portaint entre les chevilles
une chaînette d'or pour régler sa marche, et son grand man-
teau de pourpre sombre, taillé dans une étoffe inconnue,
trâinait derrière elle, faisant à chacun de ses pas comme une
large vague qui la suivant.

Do you see what I mean? Is it possible there is an occasion
when the *mot juste* can become so *juste* that it transcends even
the ridiculous boundaries of different tongues, to the degree
that, no matter what language you speak, an understanding
is automatic? Are those words in themselves a creation that
goes beyond all such, well, babbling difference, the confusion thrown up by different tongues, and glides clear into
a zone of pure beauty and significance well beyond different tongues? Is a paragraph like that quite possibly a major
achievement in the entire course of the human endeavor—
and then some?

I read and read. And once I touch back down again to
my chair (borrowed from the white vanity table in the hotel
room and brought out here to the balcony), sip another long
sip of the lemon Virgen soda (pretty sugary), I chide myself
for being lazy in the first place and previously rereading the
book in translation—three different ones in the past, including Krailsheimer's—which do no justice whatsoever to the
achievement of what is before me, the quintessential *power* in
the original French.

I leave Tunis a couple of days later, wishing I had more
time there (isn't that a given for the best travel?—just when

you get comfortable, you take out your computer-printed slab of a light-green-and-white airline ticket and reluctantly stare at the day and the hour when you *have* to depart), and out at the rather gaudy Tunis airport, a new terminal done up in what could be labeled as glitzy Las Vegas/Mosque kitsch, if that makes any sense, I remain unaware of what is about to happen to me back in Paris.

16. In a Deserted Library

In sweltering Paris (temperature records are being broken in the summer of 2003) crammed with tourists, I find a cheap one-star hotel up by the Gare de l'Est. It's a funky neighborhood now thoroughly hip, vibrant with the busy street life of Sub-Saharan Africans who have immigrated to France, their shops with names like (untranslated) "Homeboys" and "Afro King," even a standard Parisian café renamed "Motown Lounge." It does get me away from the noisy tourists, who are present in hoards down around where I stayed earlier, near the Place de la Bastille and in the Marais. I meet a French novelist pal of mine, Michel Sarotte, for dinner at a restaurant behind the Panthéon; besides having written fine novels, one once short-listed for the Prix Goncourt, Michel is the author a first-rate, probably seminal book published in the seventies on the recurring theme of homosexuality throughout the history of American literature. He assures me that even if Edward Said wasn't a fan of *Salammbô* (soft-voiced Michel has never heard of Said, yet I try to explain to him Said's stand, one most definitely based on understandable social concern; regretfully, Said will die a few months hence), despite all controversy, Michel says, the novel has today gradually achieved the status of an *indisputable* classic in France, even turning up as recently as a year or so ago as one of the texts on the sacred Agrégation exam for certification for teaching French literature in schools and universities. Claude Lévy has left town for the week with his wife who is singing opera in Metz, so I won't have to lie to him about visiting La Goulette-Vieille—for the time being, anyway. I do have one final chore that involves the unfinished business of closing out a checking account I've had with Banque Nationale de Paris for years, something I haven't been looking forward to; anybody who has dealt with the bureaucracy of French banking and its infamous runarounds and petty authoritarianism knows what I'm talking about. Luckily, the general transit strike is finally solved, and I take the RER train out to Nanterre on the other side of the La Défense skyscraper district, where my branch of the BNP is located and where I taught two times at the relatively new university there. Nanterre is bleak even in the leaf-shimmering June sunshine, the supposedly once futuristic reinforced-concrete university buildings now crumbling and often graffiti-covered, the unkempt campus virtually abandoned for summer break; the bank office is scenically located on a rusted trestle walkway over the rumbling train tracks. Surprisingly, everybody at the bank is quite helpful, and after I am first told I can come back the next week for a cashier's check covering what's left in my account, I argue. I am then told I can come back the next day; I argue in French some more. I finally get the three people who are working there to engage behind the counter in a serious, whispering five-minute pow-wow on the problem, and they agree that they can have the check ready that afternoon at two, meaning I have about three hours to kill. I go to the university library—hot and un-air conditioned—thumb through some American literary magazines in the reading room, then figure I might head upstairs to the stacks and see what they have in their holdings on Flaubert and *Salammbô*.

The tables are empty, and these second-floor rooms are even hotter. But I hit a genuine platinum mine of texts, several long shelves of works by and about Flaubert, first losing myself in a complete two-volume set of his travel notebooks, containing new info for me on his Tunisia trip. That includes evidence of how he was, in truth, very politically curious, interested in the daily stuff of administration and colonial life in North Africa at the time, F. making voluminous notes with detailed observations on the subject, even if none of that found its way into what he eventually would publish as prose fiction. Then my eye snags on a paperback on the shelf, what should be only a hokey illustrated production, an edition of *Salammbô* in a series called "Lire et Voir les Classiques": Read and See the Classics, as stated, and the *texte intégral* (unabridged version) accompanied by several inserted glossy-page sections with paintings influenced by *Salammbô* and scenes from a number of operas based on it, even stills from a Cecil B. DeMille–style Italian film adaptation—in lurid movie technicolor, the guys gleamingly muscular, the girls with bulbous sixties hairdos. Thumbing through the book, I decide to read the lengthy critical introduction, and before long I sense that I'm really into something major from its author, Pascaline Mourier-Casile. I jot down her name, because the critical writing here and the argument within are so very good—so forget the crabby opinionating I spouted earlier, cheekily bombing academics for seldom offering anything important (or forget it for now, anyway). Right off, she makes a most basic point, which disposes of the nit-picking about *Salammbô*'s historical accuracy in a single deft stroke; she stresses that while it is a historical novel, it is first and foremost an entity beyond that, essentially a *novel* and a *creative* work, meaning that questioning it as to historical details, or even reading it as social commentary, really isn't the issue. In fact, as Mourier-Casile would have it, Sainte-Beuve's demand of "Why Carthage?"—the civilization about which the modern world knows very little, almost nothing—is precisely the answer to it all. Because, wasn't the central quest of Flaubert laid out in the famous letter to his mistress Louise Colet while laboring over—and temporarily dissatisfied with his progress on—*Madame Bovary* at Croisset?:

> What seems beautiful to me, what I would like to write, is a book about nothing, a book with no attachments to the outside world, which would be self-sustaining, thanks to the internal force of its style, as the earth holds itself in the void without being supported, a book that would have almost no subject, or one at any rate in which the subject would be almost invisible, if such a thing is possible?

No, I don't have that Flaubert quote in front of me in the library and Mourier-Casile doesn't reproduce it, but I have close to memorized it over the years. And what Mourier-Casile suggests becomes the catalyst, because something suddenly hits me, and I tell myself:

Punic Carthage was for Flaubert, and most everybody else, no doubt, a lost civilization, a ruined land all gone, Carthage in a way was an object of contemplation free of any ties to the corporeal, the limitations of the material—in other words, Carthage for Flaubert was rien, nothing, it was nearly an abstract concept, as that haunting premise of his letter would have it, an item of airy contemplation to allow the master to create without restraint a book where literary style itself was the issue of paramount importance, for him to compose his breathtaking sentences that beat Time in a way that no simple plastification of documents, if you will, ever could, that rendered inconsequential, too, all the accompanying sadness brought about by Time passing—because a Work of Art can go beyond that, become as concrete and overwhelmingly important as whatever saving force that does actually sustain the earth, keep it suspended in the void, and with the abundance of sadness in the world is there ever a void, all right.

The idea deals me a rush of vertigo—it's my *Big Realization*, what I know full well right then and what has made the entire trip supremely meaningful at last.

And then there's what happens next.

17. Baudelaire Pipes In

Strangely, as I sit alone hunched over the strewn books at the table, somebody else is, in fact, sitting only a few feet away from me, having shown up very quietly.

Or, I heard some shuffling of books nearby, but I avoided making any show of observation after looking over quickly, noticing it was a young woman and not wanting to be caught ogling ("gazing?"), which can be embarrassing, a problem for a guy my age. (You know, I hope my current romantic interest of *suitable* age for me doesn't read this and see so much talk about young women sometimes half my age. On the other hand, it's all laudably in the name of literary honesty, right?—that being my sole ready defense.) But I do sneak a better glimpse now, and, man oh man, what a lovely young woman at that, seated on a low metal-legged round stool she has pulled up. Apparently, she is going through a few of the lower shelves in the "B" section next to where I had been picking at the shelves in the "F" section. Delicate features and long, lustrous auburn hair falling like flames to the shoulders of a black-velvet riding jacket, tapered at the waist; a lot of purple lipstick, Gothish, and strikingly amber eyes to match the auburn hair. Her jeans are tastefully faded and, the very best touch, her slipper-like shoes, again black velvet, have the tops of them decorated with tiny mirror inserts, what you might see on some twirling Hindustani dancer. She either consciously ignores, or is completely oblivious to, an older party like me, and this isn't any case of my sentimentally telling myself in middle age how in long-gone former days I might have struck up a conversation with her. This girl is a rare beauty, and any honest male learns his limitations in that arena by sixteen or so: while I might have stood a chance in striking up something when younger with a young woman like the weary German grad student, and while I did successfully meet and have fun traveling with a pudgy, buck-toothed Swiss girl in Mexico, the giggling secretary from a Geneva cop station years ago, this is a beauty who would have been way out of my league even when at the top of whatever my bungling sexual game reportedly ever was in my better years. (Ah, again such honesty!)

When she leaves with a pile of books—is she ever lithe, too, runway-model tall and strutting gracefully toward the overhead *Sortie* sign—I push my chair back, get up to investigate what she has been browsing. And, wouldn't you know it, it is the section containing the work of, and commentary on, that dark-eyed, rhapsodically tortured, consummate poetic master, Baudelaire, a contemporary of Flaubert; as explained earlier, while Baudelaire didn't know F. very well personally, he was a great admirer of the man's work. (Did you ever stop and think of how flat-out amazing it is that both *Les Fleurs du Mal*, which changed the look of world poetry forever, and *Madame Bovary*, which did the same for the look of world fiction, came out in the same city and in the same year, 1857, and both—to make the marvel of it more amazing—were hauled through near-identical court trials for offending public mores, as if to emphatically illustrate the never-ending battle between the play-it-safe, uptight bourgeois world and that of the True Artist?) The girl gone, I return to reading the rest of Mourier-Casile's commentary, which isn't quite as good for the remaining few thin paperback pages. But I know I have already experienced the kind of message I hoped for on this trip, Mourier-Casile's observation on that *rien* business galvanizing so many things I've been thinking about lately. And in an odd way it almost has been an understanding delivered, I now like to think, by the Baudelaire Girl, a news-bearing angel who herself already doesn't seem all that real in retrospect (did I see her? but I *did* see her), as what lingers about the encounter is how ethereally beautiful she was and also how damn good it is to see an obviously curious and intelligent young person like her—overdone purple Goth lipstick notwithstanding—immersed in Baudelaire.

I don't want to get carried away with it, but she could even have been Salammbô—not just her beauty, but also something about the undeniably *exotic* slipper-like shoes with the sparkling mirrors dotting them.

18. Sleeping

After his trip to Tunisia, a journey of several weeks all told and a stop in Constantine in Algeria included, Flaubert wrote to a friend in Paris that he was so exhausted on his return to Croisset that he slept for three complete days.

He soon buckled down to work on *Salammbô*, and, several years following its publication, he published what could be a masterpiece even more significant than *Madame Bovary*, the novel *L'Éducation Sentimentale,* which appeared in 1869. But after that there followed gradual decline: his beloved niece's husband, on the verge of bankruptcy with failing business ventures, wrangled from Flaubert his own family inheritance (Flaubert's father, a renowned Rouen surgeon, had left considerable money), and Flaubert's on-going ill health (including the complications of syphilis) turned worse, as his reputation as a writer seemed to be evanescing. Having been *only* a writer his entire life, to-ward the end he was disillusioned, broke, and reduced to enlisting the help of friends to try, unsuccessfully, to land the sinecure of a second-rate librarian's job at the Biblio-thèque de l'Arsenale in Paris; however, even then he al-ways kept writing, with some critical approval of his trio of long stories *Trois Contes* in 1877 and then his prophet-ically postmodern final work, *Bouvard et Pécuchet,* being published posthumously. He was just fifty-nine when he died in 1880.

Back at my family's summer house in Narragansett, alone there again, I sit down at the wobbly oaken desk in the small bedroom I've had since a kid, amid junk like old swim fins and tangled fishing gear; on the green walls are photos of me on sports teams when young and dented license plates from cars I've owned in various states over the years. I start going through my own notebooks from the trip. And if I don't continually sleep for three days, I pay tribute to my jet lag with some big-league napping off and on throughout the day for about a week, dreaming maybe of Tunis and Carthage, probably the barefoot kid under the stars limpingly running in happy, aimless circles with that holder sprouting the sprigs of jasmine making for his own lucky star, waving it around, or my maybe dreaming of the couscous restaurant on Rue du Caire and the Tunisian guys watching—silently, very seriously—the troubling TV news reports from Iraq there. I suppose I also dream of the Baudelaire Girl, though the sleep logged on the living room sofa or on the made bed of any of the different bedrooms I successively try for a nap, sort of Goldilocks fashion, true, the sleep is so deep—gulls squealing in the salty sunshine outside, power mowers rumbling now and then from neighboring houses and offering a snoring of their own, the summer season in full swing—that I honestly don't remember what I dream about.

All I know, or at least know now, is that it was, yes, deep sleep.

19. And Inevitable Decay

Maybe even the kind of sleep where you dream of nothing, let's say, not anything, *ne...rien*, as the construction would have it.

I tell myself there will be plenty of time for writing all of this up when I return to Austin, where, surely being able to use the extra cash this particular year, I've signed on to teach the second term of the summer session.

And repeatedly, when I wake up from such daytime napping, I feel refreshed and relaxed, and with great resolve, I start calling around to local workmen to line up some repairs. The place needs a new back gutter, plus the oven unit of the bulbous old white stove hasn't worked right for years, and it's time I did something about the paint outside that's peeling from the shingles in veritable sheets—high time I did something about all such inevitable decay.

I also finally get back to writing my own fiction, which, as always, feels really good.

2009, FROM ANOTHER CHICAGO MAGAZINE

WHAT PLAYS IN FRANCE: OBSERVATIONS ON AMERICAN WRITING ANOINTED IN THE REPUBLIC

It may be a daydream—and one of sweet revenge, to boot—of many an American writer.

You know, the party who finds his or her new novel hardly reviewed before there comes the heart dropping clean to the walking shoes. In other words, innocently strolling into a big-city bookstore one Saturday afternoon, let's say, there's the spotting of the first three-buck remainders, which pronounces a book quite dead before even being given a fair chance at slow and honorable extinction by simply going out of print after a couple of years or so. Yes, a daydream for that writer to envision a work, and all of that writer's, well, oeuvre, being (this will show 'em!) discovered and fully honored in France someday.

I mean, the French have never really been able to shake a reputation with us as a builder of lousy automobiles, after an attempt in the fifties to challenge sales of the Volkswagen Beetle in the U.S. with a notoriously unreliable little lump of a contraption called the Renault Dauphine (I had an older cousin who loved to tell how the shift lever on his just snapped off in his hand like a big pretzel stick). And more awkward to discuss—and having degenerated to fodder for very tired jokes, further worn out in the course of recent rocky international affairs—some will say the French didn't have the luck to offer the image of great modern warriors, considering their track record of being invaded in the late nineteenth century and right into the twentieth (I still see old black-and-white photos of those immaculate, seemingly futuristic underground control rooms of the Maginot Line and wonder why anybody couldn't foresee any everyday army, let alone the crack German squadrons, simply going *around* that reportedly impenetrable defense). Nevertheless, and despite all that, the French always have enjoyed a revered place when it involves things cultural, as most everybody agrees.

Concerning literature from America, they are known for showing a rare eye in recognizing the significant stuff, and, hell, are they ever sometimes right.

�֍

Some years ago, when I was fortunate enough to go on the first of what have been my three teaching exchanges at French universities, I was assigned a course that, much to my delight, included on the reading list William Goyen's little masterpiece *The House of Breath*.

The prof in charge of the course assured me Goyen was very respected in France. *The House of Breath* (1950) is a daring novel that on one level touchingly treats everyday life in a small town in the pine woods of East Texas on the brink of the oil boom early in the twentieth century; on another level it's a lyrical, validly visionary book-length prose poem rife with disembodied voices, fantastic plot happenings, and all the other trappings of not just what gets lumped into that easy category of Southern Gothic but what surely qualifies as bona fide magical realism—well before anybody even seemed to regularly use the term. The last time I tried to order the book for a literature seminar I was giving to my graduate creative writing students on the idea of tour de force narrative at the University of Texas (in Goyen's own beloved home state, and where said university turned him down for an endowed position in creative writing several years before he died in 1983, I might add), I was surprised to see that it wasn't in the prestigious Vintage paper series at Random House, the major publisher that had once released a hardbound reissue of it, but was at the time printed only as a modest offering by a small press, brave little Persea Books. A more painful experience was my going on to read some of Goyen's letters, which were eventually published by U. of Texas Press; I learned how later in life he was having trouble getting any large American publisher to take him on, even while he was being written about extensively in France, and also Germany. He corresponded almost pleadingly with a junior editor at Houghton Mifflin in Boston who was fighting in-house for publication of a new novel Goyen had just finished and already revised substantially at the request of this young editor, but—how many times have you heard this one?—somebody higher up on the wobbly editorial stepladder eventually intervened, having worked up a cost sheet and calculated projected sales, bluntly concluding no substantial money was to be made on a guy like Goyen no matter how artistically remarkable the work was, as Goyen apparently was told. So maybe the French were keeping Goyen's work alive.

Also, remember how it was the French who probably taught us what is best in Poe and gave him international acclaim, originally through the near-obsessive desire of Charles Baudelaire to translate the bulk of his work, not long after a time when for many Americans the sickly, impoverished Poe was last heard of, if heard of at all, in a Baltimore gutter, unceremoniously dying in that city and buried in an unmarked grave. And remember that Faulkner himself, without doubt America's giant of twentieth-century novelists, once had to be rescued from impending obscurity largely through the critical interest of the French.

All of which has gotten me trying to figure out this whole business of what the French do choose to anoint. I should announce beforehand that I am but a curious observer and no real expert. I will give a warning, as well, that the reasons forthcoming may portray a situation not entirely pure or even as on-the-level as may be assumed by that remaindered sad-sack author dreaming of someday being decorated with the little ribbon of a *chevalier* (or whatever the name of that honor is) in a drawing room of the frilled Élysée Palace (or wherever that kind of ceremony does, in fact, go on).

$$\infty$$

I know already what you're saying to yourself. If the French are such cultural arbiters, what's the deal on their Jerry Lewis thing? A perfect place to begin.

It should be emphasized that the popularity of, with no small measure of reverence for, Jerry Lewis in France isn't merely a gag. I have gone into the cinema section of book-stores, and right along with serious studies on Goddard and Truffaut there can be several books of similar scholarly consideration of Jerry Lewis; I have been cornered during a Parisian dinner party by a highly regarded French film scholar who openly rhapsodized to me about him. I even remember being in Paris when the movie *The King of Comedy* was to be aired on French TV for the first time; the buildup to the event was substantial, with ads on the channel all week for it, as one rainy November evening the population seemed to settle in en masse for what was to be a ritual of just viewing what is admittedly a very uncharacteristic, darkly harrowing Lewis film done by Scorsese. Jerry's standing, of course, rests primarily on roles that employ his particular trademark brand of slapstick humor, starting with a string of hits when teaming up with Dean Martin and having to include foremost his own solo tour de force, *The Nutty Professor*. When I once teasingly asked a buddy of mine, no less than a French theoretical physicist himself, to try to explain the fascination of his people with a guy who most Americans saw as—to borrow from another comedian's film title—an outright jerk, my friend couldn't have dealt me a more revealing answer, even if it was intended as a put-down. To enjoy the full effect here you have to try to hear a voice speaking in acquired English, and I'll supply the cheesy, yet I trust effective, accent:

"We like Je-ree Lew-ees bee-cause he ees so Am-er-ree-can."

As they say, "*Touché!*" and then some.

Ultimately revealing, too, because when you think of it, Jerry Lewis in his major comedy roles (set aside here the deconstructing of his persona as a celebrity in a later film like

The King of Comedy) is an exaggeration of the good-heart-
ed, well-meaning, innocent, anything-but-suave package
that does often define the prototypical everyday American,
vaguely jerkish.

On a more recent trip to teach in France, I walked into an
empty classroom to sit down and enjoy a lunch I'd packed,
and I noticed the room had been freshly decorated with a
mural on the rear wall that I hadn't seen before. This was at
Université Paris X-Nanterre, a relatively new American-style
campus just beyond the skyscrapers of the La Défense business
district on the western edge of the city. (I've been a visiting
faculty member at the university at Nanterre twice, and my
other time teaching in France was a semester at Université
Paul Valéry, part of the sprawling university system in sunny Montpellier on the Mediterranean and an ancient seat of
learning where notables like Rabelais and Nostradamus once
studied.) It seems that in adorning a classroom for Études
Anglo-Américaines—British and American Studies, covering literature and culture—the mural was true to the spirit
of the departmental name in devoting half the wall to scenes
from America and the other half to scenes from the U.K. In
bright colors on the American side stretched a collage of,
from left to right: a frontier locomotive; a steamboat; a Colt
six-shooter; a big Confederate flag; a fan of playing cards
and some rolled dice, complete with scattered greenbacks; a
hot dog (actually, more like a French *saucisse* sandwich, sort
of a pig-in-a-blanket deal); a guy with sideburns playing a
guitar on a rickety country porch; bowling pins; a motel; a
cluster of skyscrapers; a drive-in movie screen; and a black-
and-white police car. The icons are clichéd and ridiculously
stock, but, you have to admit, they are *so* American. (Also,

to show that such sentiment was rather simplistic for at least one French student during those uneasy Iraq War times, when anti-American feeling ran high, this wag wielding a felt marking pen had managed to draw the outline of a hooded Klansman above the Confederate flag, with a label on his sheet saying "USSA"; the top of the police car was scrawled over with the word "Murderers." I won't go through the imagery on the U.K. side of the mural, except to say that it hadn't fared much better at the hand of the felt-marker *citoyen*; there, part of the easy symbolism of the artist was a depiction of the Beatles and in front of them a bulb-haired girl dancing in a classic and very scant Carnaby Street miniskirt—certainly *no* need to detail the inserted salacious commentary on that—and right over the image of gray Windsor Castle, the black scrawl of the marker shouted: "Free Ireland!") In other words, I think the cardinal rule of what the French take to is what they see as, true, *so* American.

More specifically, what interests the French, as the mural shows—in the stars-and-bars banner, the steamboat, the Mississippi River gambling paraphernalia, the guy on the down-home porch with a guitar—has often tended to be the American South, which, when you think of it, sometimes does provide an exaggeration of everything American.

Faulkner was a Southerner, Poe too. Georgia novelist Erskine Caldwell has been adopted by the French, the subject of serious criticism, while it might be tough to find anybody in the U.S. today remembering more than the title of his steamy 1932 novel *Tobacco Road*. And, for that matter, Goyen from Confederate East Texas was very much a Southerner, and if not included on French reading lists for general courses in the modern American novel, he has been featured on those for classes in "*Littérature du Sud*," the title, in fact, of the course I taught at Nanterre mentioned earlier. Actually, a strange and intriguing application of this Southern fascination made for one of the great modern-day literary hoaxes in France, when jazz musician/writer Boris Vian in 1946 had a notorious bestseller called *J'irai cracher sur vos tombes* (I will spit on your graves), supposedly produced by an American, with Vian using the pseudonym Vernon Sullivan; a cartoon of Southern backwoods decadence and mock-Faulknerian intrigue, it was immediately greeted by many Parisian critics as an important new American work in translation, before rumors started to build and Vian had to finally step in and admit to authorship. In university librar-ies in France, I've noticed that *The Sewanee Review* and *The Southern Review* appear to be staples when it comes to period-ical holdings, more so than even *The Paris Review* (founded in Paris and later operating out of George Plimpton's apart-ment building in New York City, a journal that is definitely more au courant than either of those other two publications, especially—how should one politely say this, without calling it completely hidebound?—the *over*traditional *Sewanee Re-view*, with *The Paris Review* today always ranked among the most influential and esteemed American literary magazines); a major French scholarly journal called *Delta*, recently de-funct, was issued from the university at Montpellier and was originally founded with an emphasis on the examination of American Southern literature.

Not that being American always means being Southern, and there are the skyscraper and the police car in the mu-ral, other accepted icons of America that attract the French as well, allowing for a more urban experience, which often provides the subject in works by our leading contemporary Jewish novelists. In academic circles in France, when it comes to these writers, Malamud seems to hold his own with Bellow, is studied much more than Roth. Of course, in the U.S. Malamud seldom is read at universities anymore, while Bellow with his sheer dazzlement with words (does *any* recent writer in America produce a better sentence than Bellow?) and Roth with his sheer unpredictable outrageousness, his never-ending verve that can make every new book somehow more daring than the last, both are studied. But more than the other two, Malamud frequently addresses what can be the painfulness of race relations in America head-on (*The Tenants* primarily, plus some of the stories), and, sad to say, the French automatically assume that unmitigated racial tension is an entity *so* American, too. By the way, while we may have forgotten John Dos Passos and his energetic cataloguing of the wide panorama of American life in his fine *U.S.A.* trilogy, he has never really gone out of fashion among French academics.

�֎

But it's not just the "so American" element, certainly. Other factors may be as, or even more, important. Two cases of anointing that nicely get at these other issues entail the keen interest in the late John Hawkes, and, more recently, Paul Auster.

France has always been a place where literary experiment is not only tolerated but encouraged. Don't forget that it was this atmosphere that lured an entire generation to

Paris in the twenties, attracting its share of Americans and British, also one very notable Irishman, needless to add. While American publishing has probably from the start been closely, and hopelessly, shackled to what America is really all about (yes, money and the shabby commercialism it engenders, a situation that Hawthorne and Melville themselves complained of), the tenor in France is surely different—the idea of Art with the old capital *A* has seldom been challenged; rather than large conglomerates controlling close to all publishing, one of the most respected publishers—to some *the* most respected—remains a smaller independent operation principally devoted to the cutting edge and with no overtly commercial fare, Éditions de Minuit. The spirit of this has long been infectious, and in a twelve-item list called "Proclamation" that introduced the premier issue of the expatriate Paris-based journal *Contact* in 1928 (contributors to it including Hart Crane, Hemingway, and Joyce during the writing of *Finnegan's Wake*, along with his promoting lieutenants), the final four items seem to aptly summarize:

9. We are not concerned with the propagation of sociological ideas, except to emancipate the creative elements from the present ideology.
10. Time is a tyranny to be abolished.
11. The writer expresses, he does not communicate.
12. The plain reader be damned.

Or, to paraphrase a line in one of the who knows how many Surrealist manifestos from the time: "If writing makes sense, it's journalism not art."

Lately, I myself made it a point to carefully reread through much of John Hawkes, probably our own leading modern surrealist in fiction, and the absolute integrity of his experiment is most impressive. Through a fullness of language marked by a heightened sense of color and startling metaphor, Hawkes, in his peak period of production, moves amid semi-hallucinatory landscapes as diverse as Nazi Germany, the London horse racing world, and the desert American West. (The last of these is a second novel, *The Beetle Leg,* his sole major experimental work set entirely in the U. S. Nevertheless, if not in geography then in temperament, Hawkes is "so American," with his outsider's stance that bucks the ruling popular norm—call such rebellion "radical innocence"—an offbeat, New World something that does mark an attribute most distinctive in the American literary character: i.e., not only Poe and Faulkner, but outsiders Dickinson, Whitman, and Melville, too.) Hawkes seldom provides an easy read, in his earlier, loosely plotted fiction, anyway; he purposefully blurs for startling nightmarish effects, and work like his has more than once been ridiculed here as just claptrap, Hawkes himself falling prey to such treatment in extended form, I remember, by one of those young critics who have perennially come along to try to make a name for themselves by noisy bashing, typically in the conservative-camp house organs like *Commentary* or *The New Criterion.* Hawkes's best writing is, in truth, usually a very difficult prose, not at all aimed at the "plain reader"; as it near always loudly announces right on the first page: Let such species indeed be damned! Which doesn't bother the French, and in their tradition that produced the valiant, ultra-experimental schools of the Nouveau Roman in the fifties and then Oulipo after that, difficulty, and making the reader work a little for the big payoff, is often exactly what the whole point of authentic literary art entails. I personally can't recall anybody in my own English department at the University of Texas—which might have the largest faculty of literature professors of any institution in the country—teaching Hawkes, who received considerable scholarly attention in the U. S. early in his career, though fell out of favor later on, faring not much better than Goyen; Hawkes's last book to be published before he died, *An Irish Eye,* was given but a stubby and tepid paragraph on *The New York Times Book Review*'s "Books in Brief" page. Or, nobody had taught Hawkes at UT until two years back, when a professor from Paris came to Austin on exchange. He assigned *Second Skin,* among Hawkes's most challenging novels, to an undergraduate class, and he told me later that the students, who maybe had had their fill of the easy realism of so much currently "in" American writing, from Richard Ford to Amy Tan, loved the essential difficulty of it.

As a note, I might insert here that from my observation, the recent boom in American multicultural writing hasn't impressed the French intelligentsia to any great degree, or it hadn't when I was there. It could be that in its complexity it doesn't reduce itself to the easy clichés as depicted in the mural I spoke about, even though I'd argue that more than anything the basic idea of multiculturalism is intrinsically and wonderfully American; or it could be that the straightforward narration and sentimental approach in many (surely not all) such works, which could often bring Oprah to crocodile tears, come across as so old-fashioned and utterly traditional—read "bourgeois"—that outside of celebrating writers of substantial, proven verbal and structural prowess like Toni Morrison, the French appear not to have whole-heartedly taken to it. Meanwhile, the usual suspects of dazzling sixties and seventies experimenters are still those who frequently constitute contemporary American reading lists at French universities—Pynchon, Gass, Bartheleme, Gaddis, Coover, and Hawkes—and when I asked one professor at Nanterre how she could put together a course reading list of contemporary American work that didn't include at least one female author or somebody of color, I got a dismissing look that seemed to say that I was an adult, wasn't I, and I should know better—that *literature* is not *sociology*; the exchange put me in the role of just an American jerk, Jer-ee Lew-ees's doppelganger, all right, standing there lost in the haughtily named Salle des Professeurs, a ramshackle faculty lounge and mailroom. Anyway, getting back to Hawkes, today in France his reputation remains quite solid, but it becomes trickier with another experimenter—or apparently an experimenter—Paul Auster.

To be frank, it's very complicated, a case that shows how the French attitudes, which up until this stage in my admittedly random personal observing seem pretty logical, to the point of easy predictability, can possibly backfire.

Let me explain.

$$\text{✿}$$

In a gracefully written 1957 book-length study called *The French Face of Edgar Poe*, Patrick F. Quinn analyzes Gallic fervor for Poe; in an opening chapter called "But What Do They See in Him?" he talks of an explanation expressed by writer Laura Riding and notes:

The essential clue to this, according to Laura Riding, is that Poe always preserved a very respectful attitude towards French culture, and the French have been gracious enough to return the compliment. The two Poe heroes who are preeminently perspicacious and logical men, Dupin and Legrand, are endowed by Poe with French ancestry so that their intellectual clarity may seem the more plausible. Poe had, seems to have had, a wide acquaintance with and a warm appreciation of French literature and philosophy, and by using, for the most part correctly, a good many French words and phrases, he offered the best credential the French could wish to see—a good knowledge of their language.

Riding might have been onto something very fundamental, despite Quinn not giving much credence to the opinion. He concludes it simply served as a handy thesis to support Riding's own biases concerning the mustached, shadowy-eyed master of horror as, in her blunt words, "a mediocre but vulgar talent." But, to continue on this tack, it does appear to figure into Paul Auster's truly phenomenal popularity in the last dozen or more years in serious circles in France.

If at least one relatively recent book by Auster—*Hand to Mouth,* which contains an extended, maybe narcissistic autobiographical essay and an assembly of some of his very early apprentice writings—earned only a "Books in Brief" squib in *The New York Times Book Review,* and a glib one at that, in France Auster is so talked about and widely read that he has become a bit of a media personality. (I should make clear that I'm certainly not holding forth the *NYTBR* as any arbiter of final importance; however, as a writer who himself has written for the *Times Book Review*—once, which was enough for me, after a staff editor reworded about half of what I wrote, taking the teeth out of any critical opinion expressed therein—and also suffered on a story collection of my own the "Books in Brief" brush-off of the ilk that has been mentioned here, albeit a kind and praising little notice, I think I can be honest about what such treatment means and doesn't mean as a somewhat useful barometer of standing.) A new Paul Auster book in translation will invariably merit a giant advertising placard in the Paris Métro stations. I've seen an almost comically reverential article, long, where a reporter for the high-brow Parisian daily *Libération* followed Auster around his New York apartment quietly recording his every move from kitchen to study, from study to kitchen, etc., as the newspaperman elevates the day to nearly that in the life of a minor saint; a number of years ago Auster, also involved in filmmaking, was a member of the "jury" at the Cannes film festival, an entity as culturally meaningful as the big rise of exposed trestling and escalator paraphernalia commonly called the Centre Pompidou or the goldenly flaky morning croissant (among our own easy clichés for France?).

Auster had the right stuff for ascendancy. What is usually considered his most intriguing work, *The New York Trilogy,* an early trio of narratives often with detective-novel overtones, originally appeared from a small press in America, Sun & Moon out of Los Angeles, possibly indicating an attractive neglect at the time by the massive, basically profit-driven publishing powers that be in America. Also, the French flat-out adore detective novels—what they call *policiers*—and the detective novel at its best is, of course, an American form, the origin sometimes being traced back to stories by Poe ("The Murders in the Rue Morgue," "The Gold Bug," "The Purloined Letter"). Actually, the grand execution of the form—the more *noir* and hardboiled the better, replete with felt "Bogey" fedoras, rain at night in the muddy Hollywood hills, and leggy, overlipsticked dames with blond poodle cuts and rich, rich daddies—entails the kind of icons that also could have found their way into that classroom mural, along with the bowling pins and the hot dog, granting the latter *did* look more Parisian than Coney-esque in the depiction. I thought it telling that while teaching at Nanterre on my last trip, I found in the photocopy room some extra copies of the first page of James M. Cain's *The Postman Always Rings Twice* lying around, being used as a text in an introductory translation course. In *The New York Trilogy*, Auster can play a very intriguing game with the detective-novel genre, poking fun at it while taking its conventions seriously enough to give it a fresh, and tricky, intellectual application, which seems to be aiming at a postmodern metaphysical legerdemain smack in the Borges tradition (the French revere the Argentine wizard); that intent qualifies it as being at least potentially experimental and avant-garde, even if the prose is strictly straightforward.

Add to that the fact that his gamesmanship with the reader echoes a ton of French literary theory, which for a time seemed to be defining France as a land of high-tech critic/linguists rather than actual practicing poets and novelists, while the likes of Barthes and Derrida argued, admittedly quite interestingly, for the end of authorial authority, with every reader, *bien sûr*, his or her own Sun King. Auster himself, a New Jersey guy who went to Columbia, lived in France when younger and has done considerable translating of French works into English; before his fiction garnered much response he was known as the editor of the Random House anthology of modern French poetry, and some of *The New York Trilogy* actually is set in France, a location treated with admiration. The old literal French connection, what Riding saw as helping Poe, maybe kicked into high gear.

I have asked one French novelist—somebody who teaches American literature and is distinguished enough as a writer to have once had a book of his own short-listed for the Prix Goncourt—about Auster, and he said the ultimate anointing was when a novel by Auster, *Moon Palace*, was put on a list for an annual national competitive examination in France for what amounts to higher-level teaching certification in various fields, a test called the Agrégation. This is where the plot becomes as tight as that in a good *policier*, maybe as tawdry, too.

In the distant past, acceptance in France was usually more a matter of the earnest effort of a single person, often without much accompanying widespread or institutional backing. Baudelaire became fixated on the work of Poe, a figure he considered, no doubt, *"mon semblable, mon frère,"* and about whom, it's said, he told his mother that this man on the other side of the Atlantic had already dreamed his own dreams, to the extent that Baudelaire possibly spent more long hours translating Poe's work than he did composing his own in his rather short lifetime. Maurice-Edgar Coindreau, a legendary French translator who lived and taught in the United States, worked hard in the thirties to give a faithful rendition of *The Sound and the Fury* and is always credited with introducing the writing of Faulkner to France, where he was enthusiastically taken under wing by Sartre himself in a famous essay examining time in F.'s work; it was Coindreau who translated Goyen, by the way, and therefore introduced him and also many other American authors besides Faulkner to his countrymen. Today, the machinery—a good word for it, several French professors I spoke to agreed—is understandably far more sophisticated and complicated, maybe all leading to the inclusion on the aforementioned Agrégation exam, which I'll explain in a minute.

The world of those who deal in American writing in France appears a relatively small, very closely connected one, much tighter than anything we could imagine in America. In America (alas, Toto, we must be honest!) favor-trading and such does thrive in literary/academic circles, but even with gossipy, multi-martini-tipsy New York the alleged center, the country itself is so big and so messily and happily diverse—universities with established M.F.A. and Ph.D. programs thousands of miles apart, power bases seemingly everywhere, writers themselves living seemingly everywhere—that there are at least occasionally some built-in checks and balances. In France, many I spoke to were open about, even openly proud of, hearty networking. University jobs are frequently acquired through personal contacts, a lot of publishing is done that way, too; and because literary agents traditionally have been an anomaly in France (though less so lately), to have a cousin who knows somebody who works at Gallimard or Éditions du Seuil is a good way to get your work onto the freeform modernistic desk in a well-appointed office of such a major publisher there in the Left Bank *arrondissements*. Further, higher education remains mostly under central control, and each time I myself have traveled to France to teach for a semester I've received a handsome page announcing my status, a certificate of appointment from the national ministry of education adorned with baroquely official stamps, the whole kit suitable for framing. So in a best-case scenario, for purposes of this discussion, a publisher and academics interested in the publisher's American author (one of them perhaps the translator, others who may have written on the author and had their own doctoral students give papers on the author at the couple of major national conferences each year on American lit) seem to gladly join forces, if only informally, to generate interest; as said, the final coup is having the book included—via adoption by a panel of prominent academics—as the single contemporary American offering on the list of about ten texts for this Agrégation exam in British and American studies (with a heavy emphasis on literature), sort of a civil service test given along with another exam that awards a lesser certification. Which means many professors at all the universities throughout the country will be lecturing that year on that particular contemporary American writer if he or she is on the list, always a Shakespeare play on it, too, naturally; which means that essay collections and study guides will instantly be prepared on the writer's work (I had an estimate from a professor recently retired from the university at Poitiers that a student could conceivably spend over 6000 pre-Euro francs, just under a thousand dollars, on books by and about the ten or so authors on the Agrégation), and which also means that this entire yearly crop of those going on to teach literature written in English will perhaps be more familiar with this single contemporary American writer than any other they will deal with in the remainder of their professional lives, convinced that because they are now more or less authorities on the writer, he or she *has* to be important. Maybe offering a hypothetical equivalent closer to home might help: Think of everybody wishing to advance in university—and most high school—teaching from snowy Bangor, Maine, to balmy Santa Barbara, California, with lost Boone, Iowa, of the fields of shoulder-high corn somewhere in between, expected by the U.S. federal government to sit down one Saturday morning with Bic pens poised, waiting for the starting signal of the United States Department of Education's American, British, and Commonwealth Studies National Examination that will include questions dealing with ten pre-assigned books—the contemporary American literature representative being *Rabbit Run*, for example— and you get the idea: suddenly everybody is from then on a *Rabbit Run* expert and subsequently a John Updike scholar, like it or not. (Updike, incidentally, being the variety of easily approachable social realist who while always translated has never largely attracted the French academics, outside of his single surprisingly avant-garde excursion, *The Centaur*, a prize-winner there; he was understandably given a good measure of attention in the old USSR, a land of socialist realism.) Several years ago Paul Auster's *Moon Palace,* which itself aspires to dreamily scrutinize the American psyche, was included, and that appeared to be the final step in his anointing. Until something a little weird happened once the hype died down.

From my own informal talking to several professors of contemporary American literature in Paris, I found near consensus that they suspect they might have overrated Auster. Auster still sells extremely well in France, is widely read. And the popular media has been very drawn to him, photogenic guy that he is—in France, the universe's acknowledged epicenter of fashion and the "right look," physical appearance can also count, and the country has to be among the few places on the globe where male vanity is seen as normal and not affectation; I've even read that when Faulkner came to Paris the press gushed about his wonderful *silver hair!* Anyway, for some of the intelligentsia, Auster today maybe isn't quite the literary wonder he was first thought to be.

Personally, I've had my own doubts, surely finding Auster to be a writer of considerable and serious *potential* in the very original, even startling, concepts of some of his fictions, yet one who seldom pays off on the promise of the plot. He is often noticeably awkward in his handling of basics like narrative pacing, clichéd in his descriptive observation—New York street people straight from Central Casting or his Paris a somewhat tour-book Paris, that sort of thing—and occasionally a touch pretentious, especially in what seems his ongoing posturing about postmodernism—recurrent suggestion of deep intertextuality, and self-referential bending of genres between fiction and autobiography—while the product being delivered before the reader's eyes is in a style that instead of being anything validly postmodern, sometimes appears to have even missed much of the message of modernism; I mean, the narration now and then could just as well be that of standard, more mass-marketable easy realism, if it were written a bit less unevenly. Still, Poe could be uneven, too, one must emphasize, bordering on clumsy, and many times the work of a raw, exciting talent doesn't look smooth or academically—meaning "sleepily"—correct. And, above all, compared to the knuckleheaded tome that occasionally does find its way to the cover-feature, two-thousand-word-plus treatment with color artwork by the *NYTBR*—another slick comedy-of-manners novel about a midlife yuppie divorce or whatever—just about anything by Auster is pure, uncut Proust or James Augustine Aloysius Joyce.

In offering his own lukewarm response to Auster, the recently retired Poitiers professor I alluded to earlier spoke of a rush to judgment and complained to me that the French are too easily excited by anything that looks even faintly postmodern. And during drinks at the *terrasse* of a café across from the Sorbonne one sweltering late May afternoon, the Parisian professor who was actually the head of the Agrégation committee when Auster was included—the same prof who came to University of Texas on exchange and so nobly put Hawkes on his reading list there—was conditional in his remarks on Auster, stressing that when he was the committee head, with final say, he personally didn't feel he was anointing anybody as a master whatsoever but just showcasing writers he himself, *very personally*, thought should be read simply because there was something indeed intriguing, not necessarily immortal, about them; he also gave his opinion that *Moon Palace* is "the perfect American novel for French readers," the way it covers a sizable chunk of U.S. geography and culture—the "so American" element again. When I brought up the Auster case with one young guy, a rising academic hotshot teaching at Nanterre who wrote his own dissertation and then a book on Richard Brautigan (Brautigan apparently having always been quietly respected in France and lumped with the rest of the sixties American experimenters mentioned earlier), the hotshot tilted his head so he could maybe hide some behind the twin reflecting lenses of his tortoiseshell glasses, assuring me with no small measure of saving bespectacled face something to the effect of, "Well, Auster's prose is so simple that he really is quite valuable to work with in the lower-level courses, where our students' reading knowledge of English isn't that good"; it was a comment, I might add, that the head of the Agrégation committee I spoke of did smilingly agree with when I mentioned it to him. Also, in the small core library for the university's British and American Studies department at Nanterre, conscientiously well stocked and serving as an undergraduate library collection for what is considered essential in the field, I found not the expected full shelf of Auster's many works—novels, poems, screenplays, and nonfiction—but just: *The New York Trilogy* (even if it is flawed, a fascinating, admirable, and thoroughly worthwhile package, and, to repeat, his very best fiction); *Moon Palace*, which had been on the exam; a book on his work by a French critic (actually, I do know of at least a few books on him done by American publishers); and one of those hefty, and high-priced, glossy-covered study guides with essays by professors from throughout France, which had been assembled, according to that cover, specifically to help prep for the test that had addressed *Moon Palace*.

I suppose what could have happened is that in the ultimate twist and, in essence, a very postmodern way—where contradictions are the norm, nothing is certain, the assurance of smug and logical closure is for hopeless simpletons, and so on—Auster's credentials that led to his being celebrated in France were too perfect; every piece of the puzzle was so precisely in place, showing the full panoramic picture of the qualities the French savor, as discussed here, that something almost *had* to go wrong, in an unraveling that deconstructed the entire system, for a proof of the invalidity of *any* system.

(And you beloved deconstructionists of faded yesteryear, even if your inner circle went a little over the top in those official edicts on theory issued in the U.S. from party head-quarters at posh Yale, you voiced more than a few intriguing critical ideas!) I told you this could get complicated.

☙

Conclusions?

Overall, the French *do* have an uncanny sense, as backed by a winning track record, in figuring out what we our-selves sometimes overlook and don't realize is our significant writing, maybe just because we are too close to it. Though, to be honest, I think that some off their interests are often not that different from what we ourselves Stateside do take seriously and not so seriously. James Ellroy, popular here, is extremely popular in France even as writers of *policiers* go; he appeared on French TV when I was last in Paris, himself acting like an absurd parody of the hip, tough-guy detective novelist and using terms like "daddy-o" for the voiceover translation, which seemed like exactly what the French in-terviewer wanted to hear. As of this writing, my Parisian sources, who might be viewed as reliable handicappers in this competition, tell me that Don DeLillo and Cormac Mc-Carthy, each with a following in France already and two of the *very* best fiction writers we have right now, which we ourselves generally acknowledge (except for the author of a confused, much-discussed *Atlantic* article some time ago, who with forced naiveté and shameless misreading thump-ingly bashed them, along with Auster), and they should turn up sooner or later on that sacred Agrégation, DeLillo most

likely the sounder bet. One correspondent says that so-called
Rocky Mountain fiction, by popular writers like Jim Har-
rison and Thomas McGuane and their mostly Montana co-
horts, has emerged as fashionable, but it certainly hasn't yet
generated attention like that afforded the Southern when it
comes to American writing. In addition, it should be noted that the French make a real effort to translate so much
American writing. I can't stress enough that the authors I've
concentrated on here as venerated to some extent are those
who have been regularly studied and written about beyond
simple newspaper, radio, and television reviews—of which
there are still a lot in France—and it is amazing to see how
much American fiction *does* get translated, especially considering how embarrassingly little of their work makes its way
into our bookstores. And, again, concerning the matter of
our neglected authors: Set aside for a moment the unchal-
lengeable, beat-the-crowd celebration of Poe and Faulkner
by the French, and for me merely the single truth that they
created a classroom audience and in-depth study for a book
like *The House of Breath* that it never really enjoyed in the
man's own country, where prevailing tastes and values are
such that a wannabe literary maestro like the late James Mi-
chener—blatantly commercially oriented, in spite of his as-
piration to be seen otherwise—once had his visage displayed
on the side of those tan Barnes & Noble plastic shopping bags
that have also featured greats like Joyce and Woolf, yes, the
French honoring Goyen is enough for me to validate their
taste, however strangely the system dictating it sometimes
works. Believe me, if you haven't read it, *The House of Breath*
is that rare.

So for the moping, slighted novelist here Stateside, the

one who never has benefited from something like the former book-club queen Oprah's soppy praise—"These are *real* tears, girl!"—resulting in hefty sales and who cringes at the sight of *any* remainder table, adulation in France remains well worth the time spent fantasizing about it, to ease the hurt some, if nothing else.

As for the Jerry Lewis thing, go out and rent *The Nutty Professor*; fast forward to the scene of cool, Rat Pack–style Buddy Love with a rumpled sport jacket and hiply loosened thin tie trying to slowly, seductively croon a nightclub number at an off-campus bar called the Purple Pit when his magic potion is kicking in and out of gear, and in the midst of the hilarious, and deeply frightening, schizophrenia he keeps slipping into the squeaky falsetto of the bucktoothed Nutty Professor himself, a sequence that goes well beyond simple slapstick and may be as valuable as anything in the history of classic American cinematic comedy, Chaplin included.

Watch it, and *you* decide if it isn't utter—not to put too fine a point on it—*genius*.

2003, FROM *THE LITERARY REVIEW*

Postscript:

Some of the situation portrayed in this essay has surely changed since it was written a while back, but I trust my essential premises and conclusions remain reasonably sound, so I won't address all the details, just a few.

On a more recent trip to teach for a semester at a university in France—the Sorbonne Nouvelle in Paris this time—I witnessed what could only be seen as a phenomenon, the way Philip Roth's stock had skyrocketed there—which makes sense, seeing that much of the later work in his long career, like *American Pastoral* and *I Married a Communist,* does treat directly and without compromise the "so-Americanness" of things. And—belatedly, and *very* long overdue—there seemed to be a good deal of keen interest in and a most respectful awakening to the value and importance of the best new multicultural American literature, most notably that of our wonderful younger writers.

Also, granted I do argue here for the seriousness with which the French in general treat literature and their eye for what's truly lasting and in a place where best-sellerdom doesn't seem necessary to establish the worth of a book (sometimes it can mean the mark of unpardonable crassness to French readers and a prime reason to shy away from a book, actually), yet that might be changing, too, if it hasn't started to show large signs of having done so already. The old, venerable French publishing houses are becoming much more commercial-oriented, as may be indicated by just the fact that flashy novel covers and artwork for them are now the norm, rather than the simple uniform plain covers—devoid of any artwork and bearing only the author's name and title, along with the publisher's colophon—that were for years used on all books issued by any single house (Gallimard still often uses its distinctive beige and red, and Grasset its pale yellow, but they appear to be among the last holdouts), and many of the smaller independent houses are being sadly overshadowed by the bigger, ever-expanding conglomerate publishing concerns, as began to rapidly happen a few dozen years ago in the U.S., where, never mind overshadowing, most just got gobbled up or fast disappeared. I offered this observation about the changing scene in France to a French friend at dinner recently, a brilliant scholar herself who was visiting Austin, to see if she agreed, and she responded with a slow shaking of the head and a lowering of the hooded eyelids, feeling the pain of maybe the frank and honest chill of Gallic *sang froid* in the veins, if not outright, taken-for-granted pessimism, as she whisperingly asked what nobody in any quadrant of this big and glorious globe of ours really wants to hear: "Will anybody even be *reading* serious literature in fifty years?"

I managed to slap my hands to my ears before she got it all out. No kidding, I really did, looking foolish in the Austin restaurant where I performed it, but suitably expressing my own deep and stubborn and total optimism, nevertheless, which I hope against hope isn't only more Yankee dumb naiveté on this score, in a time of assaults on the printed word itself coming from many directions as we move deeper and deeper into a new, thoroughly electronic and perhaps increasingly frivolous age.

THE OTHER LIFE OF ANY BOOK:
THREE COPIES OF
MALCOLM LOWRY'S
UNDER THE VOLCANO

1. I Am Wondering

I am wondering if books themselves have a life of their own or, more so, if every individual copy of a book sometimes does have an existence, and possibly a purpose, somehow very separate from the text. I'm not sure how new this idea is, but I suspect it has taken me to an understanding that could be new, or at least worth repeating.

Bear with me on this one.

2. Calle Donceles

Once in Mexico City I came upon a rather odd copy of Malcolm Lowry's *Under the Volcano* in one of the used bookshops along Calle Donceles.

Calle Donceles is not far from the fine cathedral and regally resplendent maroon-stone administration buildings from the Spanish colonial regime on the huge public square of the Zócalo, blue mountains all around, and it's in what I like to think of as the "literary" pocket of this the old quarter of the sprawling, modern city. Literary not because of any major publishing houses that I know of being located nearby, but because there are maybe a dozen of those bookshops clustered on narrow Donceles, one after another and with open fronts and shelves so high that wobbly wooden ladders are often needed to access the top tiers. The names of the shops offer wonderful titles on their own, like El Inframundo (The Underworld), El Laberinto (The Labyrinth), Los Hermanos de la Hoja (punningly, Brothers of the Page), and my favorite, overtly invoking the metaphysical, El Callejón de los Milagros (The Alley of Miracles). I love that street.

It was a sunny June afternoon, my last of this particular trip, and I had been thinking a lot about Lowry, author of that one masterpiece in his short life, *Under the Volcano*. The novel is among the great performances of late modernism indeed, a philosophically probing, full-language symphony telling of the final day in the life of an alcoholic British consul, Geoffrey Firmin, who is called simply "the Consul"; he's exiled to a meaningless diplomatic post in Cuernavaca, the beautiful mountain resort town south of the capital and once the summer retreat of ill-fated Emperor Maximilian and Empress Carlota. In fact, being close to obsessed with Lowry's writing for nearly my whole adult life (more on this obsession later), I had once walked through just about every scene of the novel in Cuernavaca. And this time while in Mexico City I thought I might stay at the Hotel Canadá, seeing as that was where Lowry himself usually put up whenever in the city from Cuernavaca with his first wife. Lowry lived a life of alcoholic dissolution in Mexico during 1936-38, and no need to document how the novel itself is intensely autobiographical, a critical given.

For some reason that afternoon, I was sort of making it a point to see how much Lowry the local used bookstores had. I was heartened to notice that in one shop's *Novelas* section, an entire long wall, there were yellow bands with bold black lettering for the major authors on those shelves, and right between one for LONDON and another for MANN, a label surely announced: LOWRY. Not that it or any of the other shops really had much by or about him, perhaps a single translated *Under the Volcano* issued by a Mexican publisher, or a worn copy or two of the translated *Dark as the Grave Wherein My Friend Is Laid*; that's the posthumously released novelized account he wrote about going back to Mexico for several months in 1945-46 with his second wife to show her the actual scenes of episodes in the then unpublished *Under the Volcano*. The trip ended disastrously, by the way, with more booze-fueled calamities for Lowry and even an attempt at suicide, before he was officially deported by the Mexican authorities; yet it also ended somewhat miraculously, with Lowry getting word while staying in Cuernavaca that *Under the Volcano*—which had been through laborious revisions and several complete drafts in the last decade and had been submitted to publishers on both sides of the Atlantic, turned down by a long list of houses—was finally accepted by good publishers in *both* New York and London, the two letters of acceptance *both* arriving in Cuernavaca on the same day. As I said, at least there was some Lowry in those shops, understandable when you consider that Mexicans would respect an author whose most important book is set in their country.

However, when I got to one place, almost the last at the end of the street, there was something very different. High up on a shelf, but within reach, was a copy in Spanish of *Bajo el Volcán* quite unlike the dog-eared copies of a standard Mexican paper edition with its simple beige cover that I had seen elsewhere; this one was hardbound in maroon pebble-grain, like leatherette, with gold stampings on the spine and front for the title and author. Standing there in the shop open to the street, I pulled it down and—the din of taxi horns blowing and the rich, all-pervasive aroma of traffic exhaust, half pleasant, that *is* Mexico City stronger than ever at the end of such a hot and windless day—I saw that it was a special reissuing apparently for a matched series of books released in 1979 by the Mexico City publishing house Promexa:

LAS GRANDES OBRAS DEL SIGLO VEINTE

Yes, the Great Works of the Twentieth Century. And a page up front gave the rest of the good company the book kept in the series, the few dozen titles chosen seemingly free of any regional bias, listing just the top Latin Americans, such as Borges and Neruda, and showing a certain critical integrity overall, with not only a shoo-in like Kafka included, but also—attesting to a knowledge of the truly artistically significant—Henry Miller, represented by, naturally, *Tropic of Cancer.* Leafing through this Lowry edition, I read some of the introduction in Spanish, its talk of Lowry's passion for Mexico, yet certainly no extensive mention of the Mexican government's opinion of him. He was all but forced to leave in 1938 after repeated run-ins with the police concerning his public drunkenness, though he later claimed, boastfully, he had been falsely accused of being a foreign spy, as happens to the Consul of his novel; then the formal deportation in 1946 on his only return visit, when the police confronted him with trumped-up unpaid visa fines from 1938. I guess I also stared at the full-page black-and-white photo inside the cover, which seemed to be the shot from the original 1947 American edition. It showed a still relatively young Lowry with a neat mustache and wearing a herringbone-tweed suit coat and a sporty plaid tie, looking decidedly handsome in the shimmering backlighting; below it were biographical facts on his Cambridge University education and the like, but scant indication there either of the practically continual torment of his tumultuous life. It seemed odd to think that right in this quarter, the old colonial sector of Mexico City, transpired some of his worst alcoholic mess-ups while he was first trying to write a draft of this very book I was holding, which had been destined to be rejected by—even ridiculed by— those so many editors it was submitted to for so many years. I was just a couple of streets over from the still-shabby Hotel Canadá built in the 1930s, a place Lowry would himself later describe as "a nasty little hotel…like some jerry-built apartment house in Vienna or Berlin left unfinished from lack of money and then completed on a still cheaper plan while still preserving this illusion of the 'modern'"—true, it was at the Hotel Canadá and in this area that some of his most disastrous alcoholic misadventures took place. Lowry hopelessly drunk again, Lowry plagued by guilt that he had disappointed his well-to-do parents back in England, Lowry trying to get published and forever having to justify himself to other writers and friends, Lowry hopelessly drunk again.

There's a beautiful short story by his first wife, the late Jan Gabrial, an American writer and largely the model for the Consul's wife in *Under the Volcano*. The story appears to be based on events when she finally decided to leave him after their brief marriage of several years, a piece printed in the old *Story* magazine in 1946, called "Not with a Bang." Probably attracting little attention then, it has since become part of the Lowry biographical dossier and is reprinted in at least one critical casebook on his life and work. As the story would have it, a couple are staying in Mexico City. Late one evening the husband shows up in their room at what obviously is the Hotel Canadá, and the wife is already in bed for the night. He, the Lowry character, is thoroughly drunk—*perfectamente borracho*—from prowling around those saloon-door cantinas that still exist in abundance nearby; it has taken two bellboys to awkwardly maneuver him out of the elevator and into the room. He has bought a little puppy from a beggar on the street and is keeping it tucked under his coat. When he asks her to take care of the puppy, she tries to gently tell him that he has to give it back, there is no place for it in a hotel room. Seized by another alcoholic rage, he turns on her, calls her "a bitch," and says she doesn't love him and the puppy is all he has to love. He then heads out, back to the cantinas again. Feeling responsible, she dresses to go and look for him in the cold night. Finally, after some searching on foot and then a taxi ride, she finds him sitting alone on the pavement, and together they go into one of his regular cantinas, where before long he is holding court while standing at the bar, noisily and happily drunk. She sits at a table, watching it all from that distance, then remembers the puppy and sees that the husband is leaning with his arm flat on the coat that he has placed on the bar, the puppy still inside the pile of it and suffocating. She tries to rescue it, but it is too late. Railing loudly, he proceeds to blame the entire thing on her, accusing her of being forever bent on ruining him. She admits to herself then that he is too much for her, he is too far gone for her to save, and she musters the resolve to leave him at last. The Lowry character is named Michael, and this is how the story ends: "And harshly, violently, she began to cry, because she knew that the boat that was Michael had slipped its moorings in her life, and was even now putting out to the darker sea to which she could not follow him." Jan herself returned from Mexico to the United States on her own in 1937. She asked Lowry to swear off drinking as the sole condition on which she would stick with him, attempt to salvage the marriage, but he couldn't do it.

The brief notoriety from the enthusiastic initial critical praise that *Under the Volcano* garnered when it was finally published in 1947 didn't solve Lowry's problems, rescue him from that darker sea. And while most reports from friends tell of him usually being extremely likeable, even childlike and often a hell of a lot of fun with his ukulele and his impromptu singing and joking around, his life was also marked by an inability after the one successful book to finish to his satisfaction any other major writing project, more lost than ever in the pain and complications—both physical and psychological—of continuing alcoholism, complete with harrowing bouts of the DTs. His father was a very wealthy cotton broker, a stern Methodist who disapproved of Lowry's behavior and cut him off from all but minimal financial support, and Lowry and his second wife lived poor in western Canada. When they had to abandon a beloved seaside squatter's cottage they'd painstakingly built from scratch outside of Vancouver, they tried to set themselves up in rural England, Lowry eventually receiving a solid inheritance. During a particularly bad bender in 1957 he gobbled a vial of sleeping pills; the coroner in the Sussex village where it happened attributed what most likely was suicide to "death by misadventure." He was only forty-seven.

And this is what I am getting at. Something definitely struck me there on Calle Donceles, something in the sheer and all-too-obvious irony of the juxtaposition. To think of the pain of Lowry's life—especially some of the worst scenes from it played out there in Mexico City only a couple of streets over at the Hotel Canadá and environs, as explained—then to think that I was holding an expensively bound, gold-stamped special edition of the novel that only existed because of, almost could be seen as the direct product of, that torment that haunted him till his too-early death. Which is to say, there were the words of the novel on the slightly yellowing pages, words translated into Spanish, the language of the country that had once officially deported him as an undesirable, with a respected publisher in that country declaring here that the work was an acknowledged masterpiece of its century. But beyond the words, this copy of the book existed on another level, almost waiting for me on this particular shelf on this particular hot afternoon; it somehow had its own inevitability, a life of its own that wasn't only in the text of *Under the Volcano* but also in this copy's ability to whisper to a stranger like me, a writer himself who had reached that stage in his own living where he had started to have occasional doubts about the entire pursuit of writing, asking himself the usual old questions: "What does it all add up to?" And: "Is it, in fact, the *living* or the *writing* that matters? Is it worth sacrificing the former for the latter?"

Bear with me a little more on this.

3. A Signet Paperback

But probably I haven't made clear just how crazy I've always been about Lowry's novel. Sometimes it feels like I've logged as much time recommending the book to somebody as actually working on my own fiction. Well, *nearly* that much time, the whole process starting with somebody wisely recommending it to me in 1968.

When I was at college at Harvard in those late sixties, I might have held a strange record for the number of creative writing courses taken. It was another era altogether, when Harvard still had glossy emerald ivy on its red brick walls (all of it later pried loose, after it was concluded that the strong, tenacious vines were damaging, slowly wedging apart, the old stone and mortar), and a time when the stuffy Department of English kept creative writing as something you usually had to take without credit toward the set literature curriculum (which included a required full year of soporific line-by-line classroom analysis of Chaucer) or as an extra course completely. One semester a young instructor named Carter Wilson taught a section of English C, a mid-level creative writing course. Wilson was just a few years older than us students under his guidance and had actually published a couple of novels; I remember going down deep into the pulp-fragrant stacks of Widener Library, lit by bare bulbs strung along ancient exposed electric wiring, and *seeing* Wilson's books, which made for the kind of undergraduate's confirmation I needed that Wilson was a legitimate novelist, even if I can't remember actually checking the books out and reading them. I don't think booze has ever been any problem whatsoever for me. Nevertheless, there was enough of it in the sloppily typewritten and quite predictable short stories I was turning out at the time; one or two of them involved me and my Wellesley College girlfriend, a painter, polishing off the better part of a bottle of Old Crow bourbon together in the upper bunk in my room in Quincy House on Saturday night, just talking there for hours and doing what undergraduate couples do repeatedly do in a bunk on a Saturday night, while maybe the dreamily slow, psychedelically electric harpsichord of a Donovan album played on the KLH "component" stereo. (Now that I think of it, how lucky does a citizen get?) Yes, I guess there was enough booze in my own fiction that Wilson—a cheerful, mild-mannered guy and good teacher—said that I really should read *Under the Volcano,* a book all about booze, he assured me. Which is how I came to acquire the Signet paperback that I still have to this day, bought at the Harvard Coop, and that is right here on my desk in Austin, Texas, over thirty-five years later.

Mass-market-sized, its white jacket works on a motif of red, black, and gold for the title and author and then a sketch of a lone, somewhat abstract figure, Giacometti-ish, casting a shadow in front of the crooked outline of a pyramidal mountain rise and a giant spherical sun behind that. The page edges are stained red, something they don't seem to do on paperbacks anymore, and the August 1966 printing makes the standard promise of the day that it is "Complete and Unabridged," the price ninety-five cents. There's a fine, fine introduction by Stephen Spender that I myself reread—slowly, savoringly—every time I reread the novel. I do so not only for its large general ideas and insights concerning symbolism, as well as the whole sticky issue of autobiography as art, but also simply as a reminder, perhaps, of what gracefully written critical prose, with original commentary fully understanding of the magic of words and the complexity of the heart, once looked like; or what it looked like in a time before most critics—the academic ones, anyway—abandoned a love of, and even a humble submission to, the great literature they wrote about and substituted a latching-on to any trendy, usually imported "theory" of the moment, as that unfortunately became what was necessary to bolster and advance a campus career. Picking up the copy from my desk now, I see how I have carefully and repeatedly mended the worn cover with transparent tape over the years to keep it intact, a few of the pages up front having let loose from the glue binding and protruding, frayed to one step short of mummy's wrappings. The book has had some use. Besides rereading the novel on my own, I've probably brought this very copy into my creative writing classes every semester in my thirty years of teaching to read aloud from the masterful opening paragraph. It employs a cinematic panning, to go from the entirety of Mexico, to Cuernavaca, to the grounds of the crumbling Casino de la Selva there, to a specific table on the casino's terrace, where a French movie director and a local Mexican doctor are having drinks at sunset after tennis on the Day of the Dead in 1939; they begin to discuss the genuine tragedy of their mutual friend, the Consul, who was casually shot by tough, fascistic Mexican police exactly a year earlier in the course of another alcoholic episode. If there are a better few paragraphs to teach students how any setting that truly transports the reader is without doubt a matter of pure and uncut mood, I don't know about them; here's a taste:

> The Hotel Casino de la Selva stands on a slightly high-
> er hill just outside the town, near the railway station.
> It is built far back from the main highway and sur-
> rounded by gardens and terraces which command a
> spacious view in every direction. Palatial, a certain air
> of desolate splendor pervades it. For it is no longer
> a Casino. You may not even dice for drinks in the
> bar. The ghosts of ruined gamblers haunt it. No one
> ever seems to swim in the magnificent Olympic pool.
> The springboards stand empty and mournful. Its jai-
> alai courts are grass-grown and deserted. Two tennis
> courts only are kept up in the season.

And beginning in college, I myself have personally pushed the book on girlfriends, other writers, literate relatives and, of course, many students, having loaned out who knows how often my Signet edition. (On page 91, somebody apparent-ly tore off the top of that page in a crescent, the sentences truncated along the intriguing words, one below the other in successive lines at an angle, "Consul," "paddled," "hinges," and "bougainvillea"—I trust that whoever took the missing passage needed and made good use of it, what's gone from my copy forever.) I repeatedly and energetically told people they *had* to read it, realizing now that to say that to some-body is nothing less than to flatly announce to them: "You are put on this earth for only so many years, and I am telling you to take several valuable hours out of that time to expe-rience something that might make that time more valuable, richer indeed...I hope." The tentative ending suitable for that thought, because there's probably no rejection greater in life than pushing a book on somebody and having him or her quietly return it to you, with at best an excuse of having been so busy with other things lately, or at worst an outright dismissal bordering on honest enough distaste.

Which is what once happened to me after a public display of my total and unabashed affection.

In my senior year I somehow got admitted to English S, the advanced creative writing class offered every spring semester at Harvard. At the time it was often considered to be a gathering of the dozen or so best budding writers on campus, both in fiction and poetry, who were selected on the basis of manuscript submissions from probably thirty or forty applicants. Embarrassing to think of now, but I had once read something by John Updike saying that on repeated tries every year at Harvard, he had never been admitted to English S, so in my mind I saw the achievement as *very* major. At the start of the term, late one January afternoon when I trusted nobody else would be there, I snuck over to the yellow clapboard building that was the home of the Department of English, Warren House, to nervously glance up at the bulletin board in the hallway and see my name posted on the typed list of those chosen. It could have been the Nobel Prize announcement, as far as I was concerned.

But once the class started I revised my opinion about the whole idea of English S. Taught that year by a well-known—probably famous—classical translator and sometime poet, the class turned out to be far from what I had expected. Those selected were not the wild hearts who had been keeping low for most of their undergraduate days and simply writing and writing some more—fellow oddballs, diamonds in the old rough like me, I egotistically assured myself. There were mostly just the usual suspects, a predictable cast: some campus literary players from the *Harvard Advocate* literary magazine (of the ilk who often later went on to become editors in Manhattan rather than writers, a fittingly sad fate for undergraduate literary players, I suppose); and then those I had come to realize populated a lot of the tough-to-get-into creative writing classes at Harvard, which were usually taught by males back then—the most attractive of Radcliffe English majors, who just happened to more than frequently turn up (another early lesson, I suppose, in how the real literary world works); plus the one guy, an obvious and enviable natural talent, who had a contract to write a novel for Doubleday already, and *everybody* with writing aspirations on campus knew about him (to my subsequent knowledge there was never a published novel). What was strange about this class was that the teacher—smallish, hoary-haired, and competent enough, always speaking low and with good enunciation, as if he was quite used to having an audience take in his every word—did, in fact, have a separate gallery of maybe fans there; a number of what looked like Cambridge matrons sat in straight-backed chairs around the periphery of the rest of us officially enrolled students at the oval oaken table, high-class perennial auditors, apparently, with nothing to do with the university. When the teacher gave us the assignment early on to bring into class a piece of writing we admired, I produced the Signet paperback. I probably read from one of those rolling passages where the Consul—his actress ex-wife, Yvonne, having returned to Mexico to see if she can save him, and his swashbuckling British journalist half-brother, Hugh, traveling to Mexico and wanting to help her try to save him—a passage where the Consul leaps further into his alcoholic visions and transport, at the peak of it communicating with the stars and even the ages, it seems, not in the least interested in being saved, when he's honest about it: the basic premise of such ushering back into the safe world appears to him at that stage the final failure, the worst sellout. Lowry's Consul—like Hamlet and Faust and Dante's pilgrim, the personages he's compared to in much criticism—will prove to be questing after the biggest of messages as the novel progresses, Secret Knowledge itself.

No, I have no idea now exactly what passage it was, but let me provide one, the sort it might have been. Here the drunken Consul drifts half lost through his lush, sprawling garden after almost stumbling into the deep *barranca* at the edge of this veritable Eden, as he strains to find a way back to his own house and Yvonne now waiting for him there— which is to say, as he tries to find his way *home*. In his tequila drunkenness, the world takes on a glowing and revelatory too-clearness of things, and a fleeting image of the airy liberation of the soul materializes right before his wide eyes in an encounter with the cat of his stuffy American neighbor, Mr. Quincey. But there are many stresses indeed in the Consul's peaceable kingdom.

> Not that the Consul now felt gloomy. Quite the contrary. The outlook had rarely seemed so bright. He became conscious, for the first time, of the extraordinary activity which everywhere surrounded him in the garden: a lizard going up a tree, another kind of lizard coming down another tree, a bottle-green

hummingbird exploring a flower, another kind of hummingbird, voraciously at another flower; huge butterflies, whose precise stitched markings reminded one of the blouses in the market, flopping about with indolent gymnastic grace (much as Yvonne had described them greeting her in Acapulco Bay yesterday, a storm of torn-up multi-colored love letters, tossing to windward past the saloons on the promenade deck); ants with petals or scarlet blossoms tacking hither and thither along the paths; while from above, below, from the sky, and, it might be, from under the earth, came a continual sound of whistling, gnawing, rattling, even trumpeting. Where was his friend the snake now? Hiding up a pear tree probably. A snake that waited to drop rings on you; whore's shoes. From the branches of these pear trees hung carafes of glutinous yellow substance for trapping insects still changed religiously every month by the local horticultural college. (How gay the Mexicans! The horticulturists made the occasion, as they made every possible occasion, a sort of dance, bringing their womenfolk with them, flitting from tree to tree, gathering up and replacing the carafes as though the whole thing were a movement in a comic ballet, afterwards lolling about in the shade for hours, as if the Consul did not exist.) Then the behavior of Mr. Quincey's cat began to fascinate him. The creature had at last caught an insect but instead of devouring it, she was holding its body, still uninjured, delicately between her teeth, while its lovely luminous wings, still beating, for the insect had not stopped flying an instant, protruded from either side of her whiskers, fanning them. The Consul stooped forward to the rescue. But the animal bounded just out of reach. He stooped again, with the same result. In this preposterous fashion, the Consul stooping, the cat dancing just out of reach, the insect still flying furiously in the cat's mouth, he approached his porch. Finally the cat extended a preparate paw for the kill, opening her mouth, and the insect, whose wings had never ceased to beat, suddenly and marvelously flew out, as might indeed the human soul from the jaws of death, flew up, up, up, soaring over the trees...

Full prose that wears the old heart on the sleeve, all right, a rhythmic, darkly comic, semi-hallucinatory mind flow (note the deft use of the parentheses for triggered stray thoughts) that taps all the complexity of substance-induced envisioning and certainly offers a tip of the hat to the master of that mode, De Quincey himself (note the echoing name of the neighbor whose cat it is).

I've never been that good at dramatic performance of anything, but I thought I read it reasonably well that day in class. And finished, the Signet held open before me, I surely expected writing like that to bring down the house. The other students, however, were silent, waiting for the teacher's response before they gave theirs—it was that kind of class. At the head of the table, he took his time, nodded his head a bit, as if in some consternation while he obviously carefully constructed what to say, and ultimately did offer something along the lines of how when he had been a book reviewer years before on the staff of *Time* magazine, *Under the Volcano* came to his desk, though after reading it he decided it was maybe too excessive, too verbally and emotionally indulgent for his taste, so it didn't merit a *Time* review from him:

"I chose to pass on it," he concluded lowly—and imperially, the way I saw it, even if he was being completely honest.

And I might have been a kid, and he might have been the famous translator of classical Greek and Latin and a published, sometime poet, but the dismissal really stung, assaulted everything I believed in then and to this day, as far as literature goes. To ease the awkwardness for me a little, one of the ritzy Cambridge matrons—I can still picture her, an elderly Marianne Moore type with a complicated hat—did pipe in from the gallery in a dramatic warbly voice, "Lowry, Lowry, such a trah-gic life," providing some support. Though to twist the emotional stiletto yet more, reinforce the unjust absurdity of it—again, as I saw it—the next student at the table to deliver a piece of writing that she admired was a breathtakingly beautiful Radcliffe girl—I can *really* still picture her, lithe, with pouty lips and wispily long auburn hair, an affection for miniskirts and sort of ballet-slipper shoes with ribbon tie-ups—who read aloud in her melodious sensual voice a poem that I can't remember (admittedly it could have been something major, eerie Emily Dickinson or Marvell's little masterpiece "To His Coy Mistress"); the poem had been copied out in meticulous script and mounted on a 9x12 white art-stock slab with a band of soft felt making a framing border, her own very accomplished pen-and-ink sketches of flowers and leaves all around the verses. Honestly.

The hoary teacher's response, following his lingering, appreciative smile, was most positive, to put it mildly; he pronounced, "A very lovely poem from a *very* lovely young lady." Honestly.

And writing this now and seeing the tone I assume when describing a forgotten winter afternoon in cold, gray Cambridge closing in on four decades ago, I know—and it should be obvious—that the hurt lingers. I mean, do I have to call him, the much-honored man who is long deceased, a "sometime poet," get in a dig like that even today? Still, his failing to recognize Lowry's achievement, even his possibly running the risk of cutting the readers of *Time* magazine off from getting the word on it when it appeared in 1947 (though my checking now indicates somebody did review it anonymously for them), he *deserves* my venting of spleen, I'd say, which, if nothing else, stresses what *Under the Volcano* means to me.

Anyway, when I pushed the book on another party, a half-dozen years later, I got a response exactly the opposite, the variety of which any of us is obviously longing for when we recommend a book to somebody else.

To my surprise, no doubt, I had started publishing some short stories in literary magazines, had actually been given a chance to teach creative writing myself at a small state college in the sweet Green Mountains of northern Vermont, which spared me from having to return to the bleak routine of the daily-newspaper work that had been my livelihood right after graduation. I couldn't believe my good luck, granting it was originally just for a summer session and by no means a regular appointment. Living next to me on the faculty floor of a dorm was a playwright up from New York, part of an ensemble theater group, with directors and Equity actors included, in residence for the summer. I hit it off with the playwright, only five years older than me but with solid success already for his startling avant-garde work, plays done by the Lincoln Center Rep and Joseph Papp's New York Public Theater. In fact, he already had somewhat of a legend about him: linebacker big and a former college athlete, grizzly bearded, prone to wearing head bandannas and bib-front overalls, he had married early and had kids, taught English and Latin at a prep school out on Long Island, before he just left behind the entire package of the square life to write his plays in a cramped one-room apartment in the Village and support himself with a job that amounted to little more than being a resident roadie, lugging speakers and setting up shows at the old Fillmore East rock venue. In other words, he canned most everything for his writing, and living for a while now in a dorm room next door to him, I knew how hard he worked, a single exchange of dialogue labored over and written again and again, the exchange polished maybe for hours…before moving on to the next line of dialogue, and that then written again and again and again. Recently, a play of his had been brought out as a book in the prestigious and hip Grove Press contemporary drama series, putting him alongside Ionesco and Beckett on the shelf. The playwright seemed to have made it, and done so on his own terms without compromising; true, before too long there would be some extremely troubled times for him—big personal issues to wrestle, plus vanishing interest in daring work like his in an increasingly middlebrow, commercialized American theater scene—but that summer his situation was anything other than that. I ate breakfast every morning at a table in the student dining hall with him and the rest of the theater people, and probably right from the start I launched into my preaching about Lowry, one morning carrying the Signet paperback from the dorm, sliding it across the table and positioning it beside his plate of sausage and scrambled eggs to make sure he had it, then the playwright carrying it back to the dorm. The exchange was made.

The teaching schedule was such that most of us wrote in the a.m. and taught in the afternoons. And I suppose I didn't notice the silence in his room next door as I banged away at my own light green Hermes portable for several hours, didn't notice the time (this could happen when you were young and giddy about being able to write anything you wanted to, namely prose fiction, delivered from the sometimes sixty hours a week of writing meaningless newspaper copy), and soon it was well past noon. I figured I would see if the playwright wanted to go over to the dining hall for lunch. I knocked, heard nothing, then knocked again.

"Yeah." His voice was deep and gravelly, soft right now.

"It's Pete," I said. "I'm going to lunch."

"Pete, come on in."

I opened the door to the dim little cinderblock cubicle. The curtains were drawn against the midday July glare outside, and dressed in his bib-fronts and T-shirt, his Chuck Taylors kicked off, he was sitting stretched out on the bed, a sizable man. A dorm pillow propped his back, and a single desk lamp glowed a yellow cone of light over his shoulder and onto a book, my Signet paperback; in his huge hands he cradled it gently, like a dove, maybe. He looked disoriented by my interruption.

"I see you're reading the book," I said.

He must have been going at it all morning, for the four hours or so since he'd gotten back from breakfast, reading instead of writing, because when he carefully placed a ballpoint pen to mark his spot, I noticed he was halfway through the near four hundred pages. Still on the bed, he looked at me, the voice not just deep and gravelly and soft but dead serious, too, and very slow, so honest he could have been speaking more to himself than to me. He said:

"I've been reading this book all my life."

Which has always struck me, ever since, as the ultimate triumph in that scenario of recommending a book to somebody, the iconic affirmation. And whoever I have tried to tell about the book after that (I just pushed it on a guy in my department last week, a twentieth-century-novel scholar who confessed he was embarrassed for *not* having read it, promised he would go through it, studiously, as an upcoming summer project) has never been able to give such a response, one that also gets smack at this matter I've been wondering about: Again, there is the Signet paperback that contains, "Complete and Unabridged," that handsome prose and the tale of the last day of the dipsomaniacal Consul's life in 1938, but there is also this same Signet paperback, an object that I have often used to say what I can't say myself, that has made for a message in itself that I can physically hand to somebody and beat what becomes more and more as I get older the troubling frustration—or huge pure futility?—that Baudelaire defined well in the second of his two published introductions to *Les Fleurs du Mal*, "the appalling uselessness of trying to explain anything whatever to anybody whatever."

And that seems to be very much the other life of that copy, the specific purpose in my own life of the worn-soft, falling-apart Signet paperback.

4. Where Words Go

One night recently, in a bar here where I live and teach here in Austin, Texas, now, I got to talking to a painter I know, a guy whose canvases sell well both in the U.S. and internationally. He is an avid reader, and he spoke to me of a long-time affection for Lowry's work. As he put down his fresh, syrupy black Guinness pint after a first long sip, he looked up from under the visor of his baseball cap and told me outright:

"I've once even held the manuscript. I mean, it was wild, having it right there in my hands."

"You've got to be kidding," I said.

"No, see for yourself. Right over at the HRC."

The HRC is the rare books and manuscript library at the University of Texas. And I have been on the university's faculty for almost twenty-five years, admittedly an academic low-profiler in my English department, being a so-called creative writer. My cluttered office with cracked yellow plaster walls on the first floor of Parlin Hall actually looks out to the HRC. Located in a massive reinforced-concrete rise from the 1970s—a blank limestone veneer and somewhat in the style of an imposing Soviet mausoleum—the library was founded by a past university president and systems chancellor, the controversial Harry Ransom; his critics said he called it the Humanities Research Center, or HRC, possibly with the dreams of grandiosity that haunt too many ego-inflated, big-university administrators, knowing that eventually the name of this HRC could deftly be changed to the Harry Ransom Center—which it was. And there I was, a confirmed *Under the Volcano* addict to match any *Under the Volcano* addict, I liked to think, and for close to twenty-five years I had been in an office just a few hundred feet away from the original manuscript, but I had no idea of that. For some reason I felt beyond embarrassed, positively ashamed, and I mumbled some face-saving excuses to the painter as I confessed, no, I never had seen it.

In my defense here, I should say that by choice I've pretty much avoided that rare books and manuscript library. I head over there only when a reading or talk by a visiting writer is held in one of its quite sumptuous upstairs meeting rooms, with their Oriental rugs and good furniture and cut-glass decanters for sherry at receptions. For me, there's a certain off-putting, precious atmosphere surrounding the place, not only in the fetishization—as collectible objects—of books and an author's personal trappings (Arthur Conan Doyle's eye-glasses, Gertrude Stein's cape, etc.), but also in the message of how money, and plenty of it, can buy all of that and put it in surroundings possibly posher than most anything else on what often appears a very posh campus, its hefty endowment originally coming from substantial oil-property holdings. The library seems to endlessly host literary "events" and "galas," some very lavish and with deep-pocketed donors festively abounding; over the years, you might have mistaken—by the mode of attire—more than one of the HRC directors and top curators for a bank executive or corporate lawyer, a mover and shaker rather than an academic. It could be that from the angle of somebody who actually writes, it's not always that easy to see what a lot of HRC activity has to do with anything in the bigger scheme of genuinely important literary concerns, other than continuing to stoke up money to buy more, well, "things." Yet I know there's no denying the inherent value of studying an author's manuscripts and papers, and I—all grouchy criticism above notwithstanding—certainly wanted to touch the Lowry manuscript, examine it myself, a piece of my literary True Cross, I suppose.

One thunderstorming morning last summer, I went over there to track down the manuscript. I had to get a special buff card issued in my name, then go into a glass-walled cubicle and watch a five-minute instructional video on how to request and subsequently handle manuscripts, narrated in an even-toned voice that sounded like that from one of those schoolyard-safety films or such we were bombarded with as kids in the fifties. I must say the librarians on duty proved most accommodating, totally encouraging. And there in the spacious, well-appointed main reading room, the two boxes of Lowry holdings were delivered on a cart pushed by an undergrad work-study student who had taken a class from me the semester before, a smiling guy wearing a backward rapper's cap who still seemed gushingly grateful for the B that I had given him. I sat at a table under the gaze of corny bronze busts of everybody from John Steinbeck to George Bernard Shaw, and I began my examination according to the rules.

Security was understandably tight. There were the uniformed campus cops I had passed down in the lobby, monitoring a large panel of state-of-the-art electronic surveillance screens, and there was now the restriction that I was allowed to take notes only with the single brand-new, sharpened yellow Number 2 with a fresh pink eraser issued to me, using the one sheet of note paper that had been stamped, to certify I had brought it in and could take it out again. According to the instructional film, you were supposed to leave all manuscript material except specifically what you were using on the cart in front of the long, low counter the several librarians sat behind, taking only what you needed to a table for examination, item by item. The manuscript was in four cloth-covered, orange-red binders, a small white label on the spine of each bearing the title and binder number; the card catalogue said this was a "composite manuscript," and the very yellowing pages, often with the ghostly rust imprints of paperclips at the top from where probably notes had once been attached, were each encased in a plastic sleeve.

And there *was* a rush to just being this close to the artifact, seeing the neat typing (apparently Lowry's second wife, the detective novelist Margerie Bonner, performed that part of the job when they lived in the squatter's cottage in Canada) and the profuse pencil notes. The notes sometimes filled the margins or sometimes blanketed the entire back of a page, ideas on cuts and expansion, more revisions still. It all established a sense of utterly hard and utterly long and ceaseless labor; I knew it was tough indeed to imagine how Lowry worked on this book, how he questioned himself at every turn, longed only for perfection. And I might insert here as evidence two quotes I have on hand concerning how he went as far as frankly and repeatedly apologizing to his agent Harold Matson in New York for giving Matson an imperfect, therefore unsalable, manuscript; the quotes are from letters in a volume of Lowry's selected correspondence, and the first is dated March 1941:

> I'm sorry I've only given you further disappointments with "Under the Volcano," so far, and it may be that the adverse conditions under which the book was finally written influenced me to think it was an artistic triumph when it was only sort of a moral one.... So I am rewriting it.

And later, Lowry, still not satisfied when writing to Matson in June 1942, but obviously deep in the near-transcendent throes of work once more:

> But I shan't trouble you again until I have reduced the risk of being a strain on the petty cash department to a

minimum. I promise you this: something really good is on the wing this time, sans self deceptions, from this side.

Yes, perfection was the *single* goal, nothing short of it, as—alcohol problem or not—Lowry always kept *writing*. And in the HRC, I soon figured out that this "composite manuscript" was exactly that, a pieced-together draft and one of the who knows how many Lowry wrote (scholars usually indicate four basic versions) over the ten years or so he worked on the novel, roughly between 1936 and 1945. As a kind of exercise, or prayer-like invocation, I read and silently mouthed the syllables of the opening sentence, which comes before that descriptive passage I quoted earlier—"Two mountain chains traverse the republic roughly from north to south, forming between them a number of valleys and plateaus"—then I examined closely, several manuscript pages later, how Lowry had penciled in with large letters the old Indian name he uses for his fictionalized Cuernavaca in the novel, drawing a box around it, identical to the way it occurs on page 34 of my Signet, to reproduce the image of the sign on the town's tiny railway station:

$$\boxed{\textbf{QUAUHNAHUAC}}$$

I kept leafing through the pages in the protecting plastic sleeves.

Those wild early summer Texas thunderstorms must have been booming outside, but in this fortress of thick, thick concrete I didn't hear them. And I must have been in there for a couple of hours, looking at the orange-red binders, one after another, marveling some more at the amount of *sheer work* that went into the composition, some pages typed, some handwritten, notes and notes and more notes, Lowry pondering, weighing, reconstructing everything everywhere...until I got to the last binder, where after a while none of it was typed whatsoever, simply Lowry's own holograph pencil writing on the yellowing sheets, with more imprints of rusted paperclips—the novel's ending was there, but the last fifty or sixty pages were completely in pencil. Which is what was maybe most significant for me, because somehow with this "composite manuscript" going from the typing of the early chapters to the faded gray penciling of the later ones, the diminishing progression seemed to take a stand against all the rather overdone emphasis on the corporeality of books that this swank HRC stood for; it whispered the larger phenomenon of the words themselves nearly moving toward the final step and evanescing away from corporeality altogether, going into some cleaner, clearer, definitely purer realm, back to the limitless and awe-inspiring invisibility of the imagination unshackled, that place where art's Secret Knowledge does reside.

The other life of this copy of the book, the manuscript itself, was somehow to speak to anybody who carefully looked at it, pored over it, to tell that somebody something very important. And I pictured it speaking to not just a vaguely able writer like me, occasionally uneasy about his own calling at this aforementioned later stage (a bit of age brings telling honesty, if nothing else), but possibly to a rare and hauntingly obsessed younger writer with a gift and potential worthy of Lowry's inspiration—I saw it speaking specifically to him or her and affirming that all *wasn't* lost in the sacrificing of the living for the writing, the conundrum that the edition I came upon in Calle Donceles in Mexico City seemed to pose, a point that might be applied, as well, to my dear longtime friend, the fine playwright who also put himself through so much. I saw it convincing this imagined younger writer to keep at it, no matter what the personal cost; the results might be astounding and the adversity—and pain—might even prove the subject of the art.

Or, to put it another way, this manuscript of *Under the Volcano* seemingly had most everything of the final version of the novel within the four ever-so-neat, orange-red binders (I've since learned in a bibliography that it is the only existing reasonably complete manuscript, the fourth draft and very close to the published novel), it contained more or less the full text, but it also possessed an other life very much its own.

Not an entirely new idea, as I admitted early on, but its implications can become nothing short of staggering, in my opinion, anyway.

5. Because Maybe

I mean, look at it still another way, the real heart of the matter, going well beyond everything I've tried to say here.

Because maybe, just maybe, there *is* an entity in this world thoroughly magnificent and thoroughly indescribable, and it's called *Under the Volcano*.

2005, FROM *TIN HOUSE*

WORLD LIT—
MY EARLY CLASSES

1. JAMAICA, 1976

2. CAMEROON, 1979

3. IRELAND, 1971

—————— ✃ ——————

1. JAMAICA, 1976: HOW FAR THE POET'S WRIT RUNS

The actor Sir Alec Guinness once said jokingly that he struck from his travel list any country in which his friend Graham Greene had set a novel. In Guinness's opinion, Greene's nose for political discord was keen and if trouble already hadn't erupted there, it would soon enough. *The Quiet American* by Greene is probably the best proof of the theory. In the novel, Greene fathomed and foretold, with his examination of one personal case, the tragedy of American involvement in Vietnam a decade before most future protesters even realized it was happening.

During a trip to Jamaica in January, I kept thinking of Guinness's observation on Greene. The week before I left, I had finished reading V. S. Naipaul's *Guerrillas* and submitted a review to a newspaper in Vermont where I live. I was preoccupied with plans for my own coming trip. So the logical way to start the review was to say that the book held special interest for me because I was about to visit a country which appeared very similar to the lush, unnamed Caribbean island that is the setting for *Guerrillas*. I didn't know then the full implications of the statement.

V. S. Naipaul is Trinidadian. According to some reviewers, the story of the novel, in which a young woman is raped and viciously murdered, can be traced to the killing in 1972 of a British woman who became involved with a local pimp turned black activist in Trinidad. But, in a way, the fictional territory could just as well be Jamaica, the other large independent Caribbean island that is still part of the Commonwealth. Naipaul does make an effort to disclaim Trinidad's being the setting by having the characters talk about having left Trinidad to settle on the novel's island. In fact, the novel's island shares much with Jamaica. A major industry is bauxite mining, as in Jamaica; cricket is the great pastime (the avidly followed West Indies test matches with Australia were going on last month); Kingston-born reggae rock music blares on street corners, again as in Jamaica.

One purpose of my visit, besides escaping the northern New England deep freeze and also doing some research for fiction, was to stop by at Kingston recording studios to gather background material for an article on reggae. A cab ride to one studio took me through the heart of the quarter of hungry children, open sewage, and corrugated tin shacks that is the West Kingston slum of Trench Town. I remembered detailed descriptions of such areas in Naipaul's novel. I myself was staying at a guesthouse in

admittedly posh Liguanea at the foot of the Blue Mountains. It is a locale not unlike the Ridge in *Guerrillas*, with
its neat British-style bungalows and its location above the
congested city center.

In Naipaul's novel, a member of a slum neighborhood
gang is shot, and deadly rioting begins. Two politically
liberal white visitors—Roche from South Africa and Jane
from London, the woman eventually murdered by the
novel's black-power leader and head of a failing commune,
Jimmy Ahmed—watch the slum burn from their vantage
point of the Ridge. A few days after I landed in Kingston,
these were the headlines on the front page of the Kingston
Daily Gleaner: "Man Shot Dead, Four Persons Wounded,
Hundreds Flee Homes...Fires Rage in Rema Area. Fire-
men Retreat Under Attack by Armed Gangs. Blockades
Hold Up Police, Soldiers Entering the Area." The trouble started with confrontations between local youth gangs.
They were said to be politically at odds as radical supporters
of either the rival People's National Party (the majority party) or the Jamaica Labour Party. But before long, the police
and army seemed their common enemy. In related violence,
a constable on duty at the United States Embassy was shot.
A BBC broadcaster says in Naipaul's novel, "...the distur-
bances were sparked off by radical youth groups protesting
against unemployment and what they see as continued foreign domination of the economy...."

I took the train up to Montego to spend the last several
days of my stay in the resort town on the beautiful northern coast. I bought the *Gleaner* every morning to read the
reports from the other end of the island. The headlines kept
tabs on the deaths of policemen and gunmen. There were

photographs of some people fleeing amid the rubble and other people looting. In *Guerrillas*, Roche tells Jane, "Yes. One day there's going to be an accident. I hope it doesn't get to that. It's so odd. When you're out in the country, the old estates, and you see country people walking to church or rocking in their hammocks or drinking in their little bars, you don't think it's that kind of a country.... People would be frightened if they know how easily it comes."

In Jamaica, I got that feeling of "how easily it comes"—in this case, how a developing country could find itself suddenly on the brink of outright fighting and confused civil war. Or, as another of Naipaul's characters says when he brings up the possibility of such fighting leading to assassinations, "It's going to be South America for a couple of generations."

The uprising in *Guerrillas* ends when soldiers without uniforms, dropped from U.S.-marked helicopters, brutally quell it to protect foreign investment in the bauxite mines. The trouble in Kingston that began in January ended—at least for a while—without outside intervention.

Shelley was a dreamer indeed to call poets "the unacknowledged legislators of the world." However, that doesn't mean that we should continue to ignore some of the best minds of any generation—the poets, playwrights, and novelists—when their fictions offer some of the best political analysis of the times. Naipaul shows in *Guerrillas* that he understands enough about the roots of Caribbean volatility to create a fictional explosion essentially identical to an actual one that happened several months after the book appeared. I suppose one could hope (and it seems a farfetched hope) that the real legislators—maybe local Caribbean leaders, bauxite industry representatives, and even American State Department people—would avail themselves to Naipaul's knowledge. His novel, finally pessimistic, offers no solutions, but he wisely probes where the uneasiness lies, socially and economically.

I can't help but believe that our painful involvement in Vietnam might have had a different character and a different outcome if more of those supposedly best and brightest administration members of the time had taken to heart Graham Greene's convincing story of how one idealistic, concerned young American in Vietnam in the 1950s went sadly wrong in his concern.

1976, FROM *THE NATION*

2. CAMEROON, 1979: BUMA KOR & CO.

I received a formal invitation.

It came to me because a poet friend in Yaoundé had mentioned to Buma Kor that there was an American in the Cameroonian capital researching African literature and interviewing writers (I'd already conducted several such tape-recorded sessions). The card was the variety of summons that could cost a bit of money here—printing rates are high in this African country and there are heavy taxes on paper imports.

On the occasion of the inaugural opening of the
BILINGUAL BOOKSHOP
The Management and Staff of
BUMA KOR & CO.
cordially invite the presence of_____
to their premises at Mvog-Ada, behind the Dispensary
to witness the official
Cutting of the Symbolic Ribbon
at 3 p.m. on Saturday 13th July, 1979
R.S.V.P.

Next to it was the same invitation in French. The bilingualism was important. The United Republic of Cameroon in Central Africa was formed from French and British territories, a rare such union on the continent. True, the Francophone section is larger and the French language predominates. But the first article of the nation's constitution proclaims French and English as the two official tongues (there are just too many tribal languages for any of them to be official) and all secondary school students study both. Buma Kor's shop would be the first totally bilingual outlet for books in Yaoundé. Established by the French, the inland capital is cut out of the mountain jungles, a sprawling city of tin-roofed houses and a central cluster of stately buildings left over from the colonial regime, plus a few new high-rises for hotels, government ministries, and banks.

I arrived early that Saturday afternoon, to give myself plenty of time to find my way around Mvog-Ada. It turned out to be a noisy neighborhood on a hill peppered with bars and record shops. Chickens pecked at mounded garbage heaps; people stood on corners and waited for the sputtering

Toyota *ramassage* (group pick-up) taxis, the way everybody *always* seemed to be waiting for taxis in Yaoundé. The day itself was one of the absolutely brightest sunshine, with a gusty breeze kicking up the dust and rattling the clumps of banana palms growing everywhere.

Buma Kor & Co. was in a freshly whitewashed building at an intersection of streets that combined patches of asphalt and rutted red dirt in just about equal part. A yellow satin ribbon as wide as your hand flapped across one open side of the airy shop. At the front of the other open side, a table had been set up and a woman was arranging bottles and hors d'oeuvres on the white tablecloth. Some guests were already browsing among the shelves within, waiting for the ceremonies to begin. I entered from the side sans the ribbon and joined them.

I was soon shaking hands with Buma Kor, a smiling, goateed young man in a rather too big suit of French cut. He told me he was a native of Bamenda in the English-speaking part of the country. He explained that besides selling books he would publish titles under a Buma Kor imprint—in fact, there were already three books to its credit. The publishing house would operate out of the bookshop premises and it, too, would be fully bilingual. Personable and energetic, Buma Kor struck me as a natural businessman. He is also a poet himself and—according to information I received later—a former preacher. What better credentials for heading a successful publishing venture?

Looking around on my own, I saw that Buma Kor had stocked a good selection of books in French, including the literary series put out by CLE, a well-known Cameroonian publisher of the works of Central Africa's poets and novelists. The offerings in English were more spotty: two or three

Shakespeare plays in paperback, some novels in the Heine-
mann African Writers Series, and a large rack of decidedly
racy fare, several books here by a certain Rosie Dixon—
typical was *Confessions of a Baby-Sitter*, a garter-belted blond
teenage beauty toting a feather duster shown on the cover,
ready for sport—that attracted more than their fair share of
pre-ceremony browsers. In the small textbook section, the
Effective English series offered by Evans Publishers, of London and Lagos, Nigeria, caught my eye. The uniform jacket
design had the expected photos of African students engag-
ing in various scholarly pursuits, at desks or in the lab—and
also, high above all the rest, a long and sleek Mercedes automobile. Were the Evans people offering this contemporary
African power symbol as an incentive for high schoolers?
Which is to say, if you study hard, you, too, can become
a high-living businessman or politico, reminding everyone
with a flashy car that you are unquestionably a cut above the
common crowd? (Note the placement of the Mercedes at the
very *top* of the cover.) The thought somewhat saddened me.
Buma Kor's shop also stocked a supply of tennis and ping-
pong balls.

My friend arrived, the polite and unassuming Cameroonian poet Ernest Alima. He pointed out some of the
notables. The man in the blue suit was the Chancellor of
the University, and the man in the gray suit was the Minister of Post and Telecommunications. Also on hand were
the Minister of State for Territorial Administration and the
Minister of Culture and Information, the latter accompanied by an entourage of his deputies. A skeptic might have
concluded that with all the current government emphasis
on promoting bilingualism and with complete adherence

to that doctrine a top priority of the powerful (or "strong-arm," to some) Cameroonian president, Ahmadou Ahidjo, the bigwigs maybe considered this a good place to be seen. But I like to think that these government types, and the professors and writers, came simply to wish the very best of luck to Buma Kor as he started out in the book business in their city—they came to tell him that they were behind him in his sales and publishing pursuits, that they felt his work would help the developing country develop something besides the usual cash crops and even military meddling for export.

The guests assembled in the street, before the front steps, where a microphone and speakers had been set up. The sound system didn't work. The huge speakers of the record shop across the way were working exceptionally well, however, and I feared the ceremonies would be hopelessly competing with tambour drums and pinging electric guitars, the African pop singers melodically wailing. But suddenly there was silence—the record shop proprietor obviously deduced from the look of the clientele that a big event was going on.

The dedication speech was given by the Assistant Director of the Regional Book Promotion Center of Africa, an organization funded by several Sub-Saharan African countries. (Actually, Buma Kor works for the center, and, as he told me, he would be tending to his duties as head of Buma Kor & Co. mostly during the evenings.) The man spoke in French and couldn't be heard too well even without the music. Beside him, waiting patiently, was a pretty little girl of ten or so dressed up in a red frock, her hair intricately braided. She held a pair of long scissors on a white porcelain plate.

The speaker emphasized that Buma Kor was certainly well qualified, though he prudently cautioned that one shouldn't expect success too soon. Then he quoted the slogan Buma Kor was using for his publishing house, "Our Literature Is Not Dead" (an observation originally applied specifically to the literature of Anglophone Cameroon, where there are understandable worries of being overshadowed by the larger Francophone side, as Buma Kor had earlier explained to me). The little girl in red handed over the scissors, the satiny yellow band dropped gracefully in two, and Buma Kor announced, smiling, "We can now enter, and look, and"—he hesitated, smiling wider—"*buy.*" Laughter and cheers of approval.

I guess I decided then that, yes, Buma Kor & Co. was definitely going to make it.

How like a cocktail party for literati anywhere were the goings-on afterward. There was refreshment. The champagne went first and fast, then the good golden Harp lager brewed at the local Guinness plant, then the not-so-good Cameroonian brand beer, then the Fanta orange soda, then the not-so-good Cameroonian brand orange soda. The breeze had at last died down, replaced by a welcome stillness; the guests sipped and chatted in the equatorial sunlight so bright and strong you could almost touch it. A young novelist, whose first book had recently come out under the CLE imprint, complained to me that the publisher had not given him a second look at the proofs. No, he said, he couldn't really explain what his novel was about, as I felt amiss for even asking—a novelist should *never* be able to flatly explain what a novel is about. A university prof who had joined us spotted a lovely actress from the national theater group, and he politely—yet rapidly—excused himself, to try to intercept her and chat her up. A noisy, heavyset man in sunglasses, a floor-length powder-blue bou-bou, and an embroidered skullcap came up to me and made sure I knew that he was the *Director* of the Regional Book Promotion Center. In an authoritative baritone, he informed me that he would have delivered the dedication speech him-self and not delegated it to his assistant if it hadn't been for another *very important* engagement, which meant his arriving late. A scruffy guy lugging a suitcase-sized "portable" radio/tape player wandered over from where he must have been browsing in the record shop across the street and, with the graceful cheek of any determined crasher, tried to talk his way into a free drink. He had no luck, having to settle for a purchased beer at the open-air La Pirogue bar next door.

That evening and all day Sunday, the national radio (Cam-eroon has no TV yet) broadcast news of the opening. When the national daily newspaper came out on Monday, it car-ried a couple of stories with photos. In a small country like Cameroon even the launch of a bookshop rated headlines, and there was no denying this particular event represented a true cultural milestone for this wonderful emerging nation, in Buma Kor & Co.'s mission of bilingualism, if nothing else.

As for me, an appreciative visitor from very far away, I couldn't remember when I had spent a more thoroughly de-lightful afternoon.

1980, FROM *WORLDVIEW MAGAZINE*

3. IRELAND, 1971: ABOUT CHRISTY BROWN

Christy Brown's novel of the bittersweet life of a boy growing up in the Dublin backstreets in the early 1940s, *Down All
the Days*, not only was a bestseller on both sides of the Atlantic, but has been labeled by many critics as a surely lasting
piece of literature. And everyone knows that lately the two
seldom go hand in hand.

Christy is an accomplished painter as well, and this summer he'll take a bundle of his oils, most of them depicting
the striking natural beauty of the rugged West of Ireland, on
a tour of European exhibitions.

Not resting on his laurels, Christy is already well into a
second novel. It's set in America, and hopefully it will become the middle installment in a projected trilogy, of which
he has mapped out the entirety in his head. And don't forget
the volume of poems scheduled for publication this spring
or the play he is hard at work on that was commissioned by
the national Abbey Theatre of Dublin, which is certainly the
highest honor that can be paid to any playwright in Ireland,
a country of master playwrights.

Oh, yes, there's probably something else that should be
added here to this success story, though Christy doesn't particularly like to have critics harping on it all the time—he
has suffered since birth from cerebral palsy. It has left him
with the full use of only one limb, his left foot, with which
he both typewrites all his manuscripts with the toes—using
an old electric Smith Corona, the bulky, well-worn beige
contraption set on the floor—and holds his artist's brushes. He
has never had a day of formal education in his thirty-eight
years, but get to know him a bit and you'll learn that his

reading background challenges that of the best literature professors anywhere.

I've stopped in to see Christy a few times on his home ground of Kimmage in Dublin. The neighborhood is solidly working class. He lives with his sister Ann and her family in the same stuccoed row house built by the city government (so-called Corporation Housing) in which he was raised, where he has always lived. The cramped living room with its linoleum floor and mismatching flimsy furniture, along with the zinc-counter kitchen behind it, provide the setting for many of the dramatic encounters in *Down All the Days*. The pubs depicted in the novel are nearby, too, and seeing that Christy has never been one to refuse a pint of dark, foamy Guinness Stout, then before long he'll have you down to one of his two local bars. You'll be sipping late into the evening as men in work clothes shout his name in greeting through the thick smoke, and it seems that seldom does one fellow or another get up to head to the men's room without on his way stopping and leaning over Christy in his wheelchair to tell him "a good one" he heard on the job the other day. Songs, loud and forcefully off-key, break out in the various nooks and corners of the smoky, packed premises, and by closing time Christy is bellowing away with the rest of the impromptu Irish tenors. After the pubs shut at eleven it's back to the house in Kimmage for long hours of conversation and poems read aloud over more stout and fish and chips bought at the corner shop.

Framed by a tuft of curly hair and a full beard, the very blue eyes seem to be the key to the genius of the man who could produce a book as thoroughly startling as *Down All the Days*, the verve of its energetic, lushly poetic prose often compared to that of Dylan Thomas—they are eyes that literally sparkle in the living room's low lamplight when he admits he certainly *never* expected his book to do as well as it did, and eyes that are determined, almost hard, when he tells you there is no room for partition in Ireland and in his heart he will always be an Irish Republican, like his bricklayer father before him and his brothers now, ready to fight for the complete abolition of the border that currently slices the island in two.

He has visited the United States three times. The first trip was after the publication of his first book, *My Left Foot*, a slim autobiography released sixteen years ago. It's an apprentice document that Christy in a way likes to forget and doesn't advise anyone reading; nevertheless, though long out of print, it will soon be reissued in a new paperback edition. He has close friends in Stamford, Connecticut, where he is a certified honorary member of the Ancient Order of Hibernians, he laughs, and on a promotional tour for his book last summer he spent most of his spare time in New England, which he loves and which will figure considerably into his next novel, to be titled *A Shadow on Summer.*

He speaks of the fine seaside towns in Connecticut and Massachusetts and the spectacle of autumn foliage in the New England hills. He says Boston is his favorite American city and, in his opinion, very much like Dublin, with its narrow streets, formal parks, and abundance of "beautiful" dirty redbrick architecture. Of course, he couldn't live in any place else but Ireland, not permanently, anyway, but he adds that he often thinks about setting up a part-time residence somewhere in New England, maybe to begin putting down on canvas some of that handsomeness of the countryside.

Another idea that has been bouncing around in his mind lately, a dream of his, actually, is to cross the United States for a camping tour by motor trailer. He has never seen the American West and he's convinced that taking to the road à la Steinbeck in *Travels with Charley* would be the only way to do it right.

He does maintain many strong opinions on his own country. He holds that the trouble in the Northern Ireland stems from a serious and longstanding economic split rather than a religious one—the old story where one class keeps another down not just for status but for exploitation and moneymaking, too. The present British-allied Stormont government there represents the Protestants, who often are the landowners and business proprietors, while the average Catholic is inevitably the working man. He worries that the American people don't take seriously enough the "grave situation" that does exist in Northern Ireland today and they still think that the fighting in Derry and along the infamous Falls and Shankill Roads in Belfast represents but a few brawling Irish rebels stirring up a street melee here and there with some stolen ammunition. He says that maybe because Americans are used to larger scale and exorbitantly expensive foreign wars, like the current conflict in Vietnam, they can't find it easy to either sympathize with or understand the kind of turbulence now starting to wrack the North.

And he believes that the Catholic Church that embraces most of the population in the rest of Ireland is, surprisingly, undergoing change, which he's sure can only turn out for the better. He sees the old-school clergy, bent on enforcing the discipline of harsh denial, gradually being replaced by a new breed of younger priests, prepared to discuss in the open the problems of a contemporary society, including contraception—it has long been a taboo topic in his country, where the sale of all birth-control devices is strictly banned by national law. According to Christy: "The Catholic Church is finally, and I mean *finally*, admitting that it has to make concessions to the members of a younger generation." He says the Church must do so or it will lose them completely, go out of business altogether. Another longstanding problem that concerns him is that the most gifted of its younger people continue to emigrate from the country to pursue careers elsewhere, England, usually, where several of the Brown siblings themselves (there were a full thirteen kids in his family, all packed into that row-house flat) are living now.

On the whole he harbors a strong fondness for Americans. He confesses to having been a fervid, even close to fanatical, admirer of both Jack and Bobby Kennedy, and he sees Ted sadly as a "man drained of spirit," one who will probably be rendered somewhat lost as time goes by because of all the tragedy that has befallen the family.

Christy is sharply critical, however, of one American custom—drinking at home rather than in a bar or pub: "Americans don't go out for a few jars." He says they do most of that drinking at home alone, or if with friends, there's the formality of inviting them over for cocktails, and even then there's always dinner afterward. "Dinner, now that's a waste of an awful lot of important drinking time," Christy is quick to point out.

Understandably, with his feistiness he has emerged as a character of sorts in Ireland. Primed with stout and Irish whis-key, he repeatedly and emphatically used one of his dearer four-letter words on the air during an Irish network live talk show, making what he likes to think of as "television history," for Ireland, anyway; after that he was banned entirely from the local air waves for a while. He says that aware of this, David Frost called him aside when he, Christy, showed for a New York City taping of Frost's talk show last summer along with his burly younger brother Sean (employed at the Jameson Whiskey plant in Dublin), who accompanied him to the U.S.; Frost sternly told Christy to *please* try to keep all obscene language in check. Worse, in the course of the taping, ever-serious, schoolteacherish Frost leaned forward in his chair and overearnestly asked him if he believed in God, which isn't the type of question Christy thinks should *ever* be posed on television: "I thought he was going to ask me next about how my sex life was going." Which Christy almost wishes he had, because, he says, he would have been happy to announce that at that particular time it was going quite well: "Better than David Frost's, I bet."

He notes, really smiling now: "I have no formal education and maybe that's why I can write." His late mother—a figure much like the selfless, brave mother character in *Down All the Days*, the heroine of the novel—argued that Christy not be institutionalized when he was a child, as social workers urged be done; she chose to take care of him herself, even if it was a very heavy added burden for her. The schooling he did acquire was largely what he styled for himself—the handicapped boy at home devouring paperback after paperback in a determined effort to read through the entire gamut of great world literature, which, like his ultimate literary hero Thomas Wolfe before him, he actually set out to try to do. He explains that his gruff and often violently drunk father maybe saw it as a good babysitting device, slipping Christy about ten shillings a week out of his meager salary to buy enough books to keep himself occupied. Christy says he could usually get two five-shilling editions with the money, and that was quite enough, he emphasizes—two books a week, week after week.

Probably more than enough, I'd say, considering the writer he turned out to be as he worked away on that Smith Corona and his lofty stature in the literary world at the moment.

1971, FROM *THE PROVIDENCE SUNDAY JOURNAL*

Postscript:

Christy Brown died in 1981.

As explained earlier in these pages, much material from *Down All the Days* provided the basis of the acclaimed 1989 film about him starring Daniel Day Lewis, which borrowed the title of the earlier autobiography that he advised here that nobody should read, *My Left Foot.* A straightforward and admittedly rather casual newspaper feature piece like this certainly doesn't fully get at the complexity of this spirited man who didn't let his many sadnesses defeat him, who loved literature and especially the utter musical beauty of words themselves as fervently as probably anybody I've ever encountered. And it doesn't get at the experience for me as a hopeful, albeit constantly cold, twenty-three-year-old wan-nabe writer living for the better part of a year in an absurdly cheap seven-dollar-a-week bed-sitter in dank Dublin, sans central heat (the place did come with a pink hot water bot-tle to warm the sagging bed, the plump landlady carefully demonstrating to me how to pour the steaming kettle to fill it, as if it were a complicated lab experiment); I was do-ing some journalism and, more importantly to me, trying to get a start on my own fiction. I valued the relationship with Brown that developed after I initially interviewed him for the newspaper piece, our long and excited conversations about books. My subsequent visits to the Kimmage row house inevitably ended up at night in our happy inebriation in a local pub along with his sister and her husband and a brother or two, with ever-generous Christy never letting anybody else pay for anything, and then all of us back to the row house again afterward for more good talk and, yes, booze, as described. But before the going to the pub, at the house with him in the late afternoon, I became almost a de facto secretary on occasion, helping him come up with re-sponses to fan mail and making note of novels he wanted me to buy for him at the big Eason's book and stationery store on O'Connell Street when I was downtown. Along the lines of the essay in this collection on Malcolm Lowry's *Under the Volcano,* "The Other Life of Any Book," and my talk there of endlessly pressing that novel on people, I remember that when I got Brown a copy of it at Eason's, he read it, loved it, and told me: "This is the book that F. Scott Fitzgerald was always trying to write with *Tender Is the Night* but failed to do." Hauntingly perceptive, all right, because I later learned that Lowry himself was nothing short of obsessed with *Tender*

Is the Night, which did endlessly thwart Fitzgerald during its troubled composition, Fitzgerald never satisfied with that tale of Dick Diver's downward spiral and personal unraveling. Lowry even spent a large chunk of his own time in the 1950s working on an intriguing, if not very accurate, film adaptation of *Tender is the Night* that was never produced. I should note that while some of Brown's observations on his homeland here might seem a given today, he was very prescient in things he said, predicting without hesitation the full-fledged mess that the renewed Protestant-Catholic strife, which was beginning to rapidly escalate at the time of my acquaintance with him, 1971, would degenerate into in the coming years; he was equally insightful about how the Irish Catholic Church, which more or less had the nation in a psychological hammer lock back then, had to start loosening up if it expected to survive. (To give you a sense of the prevailing atmosphere: Not only were condoms still strictly illegal and black-market fare, but I once got stuck on a poky train winding forever through the green-on-green mountains and heading toward Yeats's hometown of Sligo in the West of Ireland with a wacky priest who railed against what he saw as the filth in *Catcher in the Rye*; he was shocked by my liking the novel and asked how could I *ever* consider any book "decent" if it contained within its pages even a single mention of a character who was a *prostitute?*)

Christy Brown was married and living in Somerset in the UK at the time of his death at the age of forty-nine.

TWO SHORT MOVIES AND
A TRANSCENDENT TRAILER:
WITH N. WEST
IN HOLLYWOOD

———————— ✂ ————————

Lately I have been feeling even more discouraged than usual. The ancient bugaboo—'Why write novels?'—is always before my mind.

—NATHANAEL WEST, FROM A 1940 LETTER AND JUST
BEFORE HIS DEATH AT AGE THIRTY-SEVEN IN
AN AUTOMOBILE CRASH

1. Working

I'm in L.A. for a week or so, now that my semester of teaching back in Austin is over. It's late May.

Set up at a motel downtown, I'm by myself and working on revising some rough sequences in a long fiction manuscript of my own here.

2. As Good a Place as Any

I figured that L.A. was as good a place as any to get away from everything (real sadness over the past few months involving the serious illness of a friend in Austin, which I won't go into, and then the always crazy crunch at the end of a semester—grading looming stacks of short stories from students in my creative writing classes, along with a couple of unexpected faculty skirmishes, the petty, departmental-politics kind of stuff I usually manage to sidestep and the only truly bad part of a teaching job, where those students are by and large wonderful), yes, get away and concentrate on the manuscript.

I've already gone up to Hollywood on this trip. I walked around one afternoon, tracking down the actual settings of scenes in Nathanael West's 1939 novel *The Day of the Locust*, heading there after I finished more work in the morning on the manuscript at the motel—a cheap but comfortable spot in Chinatown—then I ended the day with a drink on Hollywood Boulevard. This particular afternoon I plan to do the same.

3. On the Boulevard, a Short Movie

It's only about twenty minutes, one change involved, on the hissing train of the L.A. Metro.

And, three o'clock on a warm weekday, I'm soon stepping out of the car in the empty Hollywood station. There's the dry smell of maybe dust and electricity, like vacuum cleaner innards, that could be any subway platform anywhere, though the station here is definitely not a standard one.

Clean to the point of gleaming, as is just about everything in the new L.A. Metro system, the station is actually somewhat over the top, with almost a forest of repeated support pillars that are made to look like palm trees—concrete trunks sprouting gold and green ceramic fronds—and the vaulted ceiling showing a pattern of empty movie reels; the red floor of the expanse spreads like a lake, it's so freshly polished, and a wavy inlay through it mimics (what else?) the Yellow Brick Road. It takes two escalators, long ones, to proceed through the two levels of the station—which is to say, to go from far, far underground and then fully into the glaring sunlight again.

On the second escalator, I ride the continually folding steps, no passengers except for me, and eventually do see a blue swatch of sky above. I suppose I tell myself what I've told myself before: granting it *is* over the top, this gaudy, absurd station with its bright stainless-steel escalators slowly bringing you closer and closer is a perfect way to be, well, delivered smack into the acknowledged heart of the place, Hollywood and Vine.

Not paying any attention to the gathering of touts for guided tours and the few straggling and confused tourists in front of the station, I head for 1817 Ivar Street. I was there when in Hollywood a couple of days earlier, but I want to get a better look at it now, having reread some pages in my old, well-worn New Directions copy of *The Day of the Locust* in the motel the night before and decided that the apartment house on Ivar, called Pa-Va-Sed and mentioned by West's biographers, most likely did provide the model for the apartment house where many of the cast of down-and-out characters in the novel live, called San Bernardino Arms.

⋛

Ivar isn't far down the Boulevard, a cross street intersecting with that supposed Walk of Fame.

My progress is slowed some with the gradually increasing number of tourists—always thickest by Grauman's Chinese Theatre much farther on—who are repeatedly stopping to look down. (For me, happening to notice one of those endlessly continuing bronze plaques set in red and black terrazzo on the sidewalk is never a matter being struck by the name of a real star, somebody you expect, Jack Lemon, let's say, but the whole weirder exchange of seeing and thinking about a personage you haven't thought about in years, somebody rather inconsequential in the bigger scheme of things—maybe Arthur Treacher, a name often associated with a fish and chips chain, or Forrest Tucker, a name usually only associated with—almost worse than fish and chips—the 1960s TV sitcom about a bunch of loopy cavalrymen in the Old West, *F Troop*). I turn at an old yellow brick office building, now a Scientology museum. Unlike the Boulevard, Ivar is all but deserted in the mid-afternoon sun that is genuinely hot now, and wearing black Levi's and an open-collared dress shirt with the sleeves rolled up, the basic black-and-white nylon Reeboks I swear by and have repeatedly purchased for years, nicely bouncy under my feet, I'm glad I gunked up with sun block before setting out. I can see the low blond hills beyond Ivar—the distant HOLLYWOOD sign a faded and near ghostly white, the letters a bit lumpily angled like uneven teeth—and, steeply rising, the narrow open street gives way after a couple of blocks to welcome shade from big, spreading-limbed trees along the sidewalk on either side, the lovely jacarandas wispy with their dangling purple spring blossoms right now and certainly no shortage of the more than ubiquitous L.A. eucalyptus; everything is suddenly quite residential.

I stand across the street from the Pa-Va-Sed Apartments (the name apparently came from a reworking of the Latin phrase for "small but nice"). I look at the place, then scribble some observations in my pocket notebook, remarking that while West might have changed the façade of the apartment house in the novel, as he did the name (the Pa-Va-Sed is mock Tudor, all yellow stucco and crisscrossing chocolate-brown beams on the front gable, a roof shingled with slate the hue of pigeon feathers, and the San Bernardino Arms in the novel opts for a Moorish motif, complete with swirly pink front columns, though both are basically exercises in Hollywood's typical architectural whimsy, hopefully exotic)—true, while the façade is different, the rest of it is the same: after the false front, the functional blank walls of the building's sides stretch far back for the three floors of it, exactly as described in the novel, something I checked in the book the night before: "It was an oblong, three stories high, the back and sides of which were of plain, unpainted stucco, broken by even rows of unadorned windows."

I cross the street, for a closer look. There's trimmed shrubbery and a low brown brick wall, an open black wrought-iron gate. I decide I might enter the sidewalk courtyard and go up the stairs, peek into the lobby, where I see its oatmeal walls and a frosted central skylight and a single Mission-style easy chair upholstered in red beside the stairs, the long corridors of all three floors clearly visible and the Pa-Va-Sed unexpectedly neat within (I have my little notebook out again, am writing down with a Bic what I observe); I step aside when a young woman, a brunette in shorts carrying a big artist's portfolio, comes out of the door and goes down the brown brick steps, and I do the same when a scruffy young guy, tall and wearing a ball cap, walks up the steps and through the door. Both nod to me, seemingly not surprised that there's a gray-haired guy, me, standing on their front steps beside the panel of mailboxes and writing in a notebook (did they think I was leaving an important message for somebody?). I make a note that, as in West's day, these kids who have apartments here are probably not unlike West's characters, living in a cheap place and working—or at least trying to find work and make it—in Hollywood.

�֎

I head back down the hill of Ivar, toward the Boulevard but not directly, wandering through more of the leafy quiet side streets for a while. (There's a corner place, white stucco, called the Playboy Liquor Store—I like the name; there's another older apartment building not unlike the Pa-Va-Sed, with a drooping banner out front, red on white, saying furnished units are available for $185 a week.) I guess I feel good about having identified the real Pa-Va-Sed as being, essentially, the imaginary San Bernardino Arms, and, not to get too far ahead of myself, this is the start of it all, what will lead this afternoon to the crazy scene across from the Chinese Theatre.

But first maybe a little background—or "backstory" in movie parlance, which seems suitable here—is needed.

✖

The Day of the Locust was West's last novel, published in 1939 and a year before his death. It came out while he was living in Hollywood, by then reasonably successful in writing for the movies. Returning from a weekend hunting trip to Mexico, West failed to stop at a rural intersection outside El Centro, California. He and his wife of less than a year, Eileen McKenney (a very pretty if somewhat eccentric young woman, subject of a series of *New Yorker* pieces that became the basis of a long-running Broadway show, *My Sister*

Eileen), were killed when a car smashed full force into their wood-paneled Ford station wagon.

Of course, there has never been much critical argument that *The Day of the Locust*, which received little attention when published, is the very best of that specific genre commonly known as the Hollywood novel, yet to categorize it as such, I think, is surely not to give it the credit it deserves. (A while back I read—or in some cases reread—through probably the entire canon of said genre in a single stretch, from Fitzgerald's unfinished *The Last Tycoon* to Budd Schulberg's overrated *What Makes Sammy Run?* to Joan Didion's still absolutely stunning *Play It as It Lays*, one book to at least be mentioned in the same breath as *The Day of the Locust*, I'd say, along with the British writer Gavin Lambert's hauntingly moving cult favorites about Hollywood, *The Slide Area* and *The Goodbye People*.) Actually, *The Day of the Locust* is not *simply* a Hollywood novel, and it's one of the high points in twentieth-century American fiction itself, admittedly overshadowed by West's earlier novel *Miss Lonelyhearts*. *Miss Lonelyhearts* was never recognized as it should have been during his lifetime either, though today there's no limit, it seems, to the respect it's afforded. According to critic Harold Bloom (and whether or not you like the man's bluster, you can't deny his aesthetic acumen and unshakable standards): "The greatest Faulkner, of *The Sound and the Fury, As I Lay Dying, Absalom, Absalom!* and *Light in August*, is the only writer of prose fiction in this century who can be said to have surpassed *Miss Lonelyhearts*"; probably the whole tradition of modern American black humor, reflecting an anxious, ever-looming absurdity in life, traces back to the book, with Flannery O'Connor, John Hawkes, and Thomas Pynchon all greatly influenced by it.

It was a meandering road in life that brought West to the moment of his writing *The Day of the Locust*, one with many labels to define him along the way: privileged son of a well-to-do apartment house developer in New York City; high school dropout who managed to finagle admission to Brown University on the basis of a doctored grade transcript of somebody else who shared his name, Nathan Weinstein (which got changed to Nathanael West when he started publishing); desk clerk for two midtown Manhattan hotels after his father lost everything in the Crash, boring employment that turned out to be lucky, if only for the fact that while working in the hotels he sometimes had drinks with a reporter friend from the *Brooklyn Eagle*, who one night in a speakeasy showed him a bundle of painful letters to the paper's personal-advice column and the letters became the basis for *Miss Lonelyhearts*; struggling Hollywood screenwriter, first brought there for a few brief months in 1933 when Columbia purchased film rights to *Miss Lonelyhearts*, as followed by a return to Hollywood in 1935 with no contract, West unemployed for a long stretch, broke, and living in a cubbyhole room in the Pa-Va-Sed, acute gonorrhea contracted from prostitutes not helping the situation; and finally established Hollywood screenwriter with steady and well-paid employment, first at Republic, a B-movie operation, then major studios, RKO and Paramount, before going back to Columbia. In his trademark Ivy League clothes and known for a quiet yet sarcastic manner, a wiry, military-mustached man, West did seem out of place in Hollywood, and he always frankly admitted that writing for the movies was inherently frivolous; nevertheless, turning out scripts came easy to him, plus the pay was extremely lucrative by Depression standards and the company was good (West spent considerable time with his old college pal S.J. Perelman, who wrote Marx Brothers films and married West's sister, and he developed friendships with Fitzgerald and Faulkner, also working for studios during these years), but West still wanted to concentrate on his own fiction, reaching a point of total discouragement on that front when *The Day of the Locust* garnered few reviews and sold little more than a thousand copies. It was then that he wrote to an acquaintance back East, the poet and critic Malcolm Cowley, with that large question I affixed above as an epigraph, concerning the "ancient bugaboo," all right: "Why write novels?"

Or why write serious ones that aspire to being art and bona fide literature, anyway.

⚭

At the time of his death, in fact, West wasn't read much at all. One of the saddest things I came across in my own reading around in accounts of his life was an anecdote about how Jean-Paul Sartre, when he traveled to New York for the first time, after the War, kept asking anybody he ran into there if they knew anything about this magnificent American writer whose work Sartre had immersed himself in, Nathanael West. Nobody seemed to have heard of him, though Sartre got through by telephone to Random House, original publisher of *The Day of the Locust*, and an editorial employee thought the name sounded familiar; if I remember correctly, that prompted the employee to check and eventually tell Sartre they had been forwarding mail to West at a P.O. box that the writer apparently kept in New York City—in other words, there were people in West's own publishing house who didn't even realize he was dead.

And I suppose I think about something like that, too, while I keep walking around these neighborhoods in Hollywood this afternoon—not only residential but surprisingly sedate and everyday, considering they're so close to the Boulevard—then I go back toward the Boulevard, with the mission to the Pa-Va-Sed—that confirmation, as said—accomplished.

❧

As impressive as the newly developed Metro system for L.A. is, what can be more striking is the way the city appears to have gotten graffiti largely under control (even much that lingers in the outlying neighborhoods often looks old and faded, including in Watts, where I will go during this stay to see at last the wild triplicated exercise in wire and ceramic fragments, prophetically postmodern, that is Simon Rodia's Watts Towers); also always really noticeable is the successful solution to the pedestrian-motorist battle in L.A., the result of hefty tickets and strict enforcement of the law wherever there's a light at an intersection. With nobody jaywalking, it allows you to overhear things as the bunched people wait for the signal on the Boulevard. I hear an overweight young wannabe hipster with a ponytail excitedly telling another guy waiting with him for the red to turn to green: "I mean, it's a killer song, and the wild thing about it is that I wrote it last week in only an hour. It's called, 'Hey, Lardass!' which is what the cops said to me when they arrested me that time." He emits a grunting sound for the thump of a guitar chord, also pantomimes an axing sweep of one arm to hit the imaginary Fender, à la Pete Townshend, adding, "The opening downbeat is totally killer." And then, right before the build-up at another intersection, there's an older guy standing on the sidewalk—short, lean, and gray-mustached, wearing a crisp white T-shirt and blue jeans—and he's publicly chewing out three scruffy kids, in their late teens or early twenties and all in ragged black, who seem to have everything they own with them there on the sidewalk, backpacks and duffle bags; he shouts that he's already given them a lot—a place to stay, food to eat—and the lanky washed-out girl with stringy honey hair who is with the two boys (all of them standing there and doing their best to simply look at each other, ignore the older guy) flatly and sardonically says: "Yeah, tell it to your girlfriends, Walt."

Hollywood Boulevard, all right.

✆

Of course, I've already explored other spots that figure into the novel, on that other afternoon in Hollywood.

I've been over to the location of the old Columbia Studios, just below Hollywood Boulevard on Sunset. Columbia moved elsewhere, but the walled-off few city blocks of offices and sound stages are painted a uniformly brilliant creamy hue, spindly mop-headed palms all around, for what is now the thriving, independent Sunset Gower Studios, used principally for TV. It was most likely here—an unidentified studio within walking distance of the Boulevard and the San Bernardino Arms Apartments—that the main character in *The Day of the Locust* works; he's a recent Yale grad named Tod

Hackett, a set designer living in the San Bernardino. Across from the studios, on the corner with Gower Street, is a small new strip mall with an Old West motif called Gower Gulch, built on the very site of that same name where cowboy extras looking for bit parts in Westerns—intimately known as "horse operas" in West's day—used to gather, a spot also figuring prominently in *The Day of the Locust*. In the novel a cast of males are defined more or less in terms of their relationship to a central female presence, Faye Greener, who lives with her ex-vaudevillian father in the San Bernardino. Faye is a willowy, blond seventeen-year-old extra in the movies—and briefly a call girl—who dreams of being a star and, ever the flirting tease, already puts on the affected airs of a star, absurdly but alluringly so, too, to the degree that the male characters all move about her like minor planets in a slow, drugged orbit that can only lead to inevitable and dramatically explosive collision by the novel's end. Among those enamored with her are both Tod, the sensitive Easterner who longs to paint seriously, and, of course, Homer Simpson (the popular prime-time cartoon show later slyly borrowed his name but certainly not his character) from Iowa and now in the sunshine of Southern California for his health, a nervously shy square of a retired middle-aged bookkeeper who beautiful Faye eventually goes to live with in his tiny rented bungalow—a Platonic deal, as she unabashedly takes complete advantage of his supporting her. And there's also Faye's occasional boyfriend Earle Shoop, a cowboy extra from Arizona—laconic and dumb and handsome—who daily stations himself there at Gower Gulch alongside his friends—other cowboy extras and a street-smart, wise-cracking Indian in full tribal dress peddling cheap souvenirs (he's somebody

known to fellow Gower Gulch habitués as—this is fun-
ny—"Chief Kiss-My-Towkus"). I've even been clear over to
Western Avenue, and while there's no locating today what
might have been the Cinderella Bar, a campy nightclub built
in the shape of a giant slipper and where several characters
in *The Day of the Locust* go one evening to watch a gay drag
show (Faye takes cruel satisfaction in embarrassing the awkward Homer there), I've seen how Western Avenue does still
have some lively bars and clubs for the LGBT scene.

Actually, this day I'd planned on ending up at the Musso
and Frank's Grill. It's an iconic Hollywood eatery, upscale and
on the Boulevard, where toward the end of the novel a
distraught Tod, alone, orders a steak he hardly touches
and tries to sort out his life. Musso and Frank's is now
a bar/restaurant that basks in the fact it's in an undeniable
time warp, a bronze plaque bolted to the putty-color stucco exterior (is everything in Los Angeles stuccoed?) saying
"Est. 1919." Just the overpriced look of the place from outside now deters me from my original idea of having a drink
there; on my other afternoon in Hollywood, I discovered
a small bar called the Powerhouse right on Highland and a
block up from the Boulevard with surprisingly cheap bottles of Budweiser, more my kind of venue and an agreeable
watering hole that if it's iconic of anything it could be the
life and times of Charles Bukowski—I figure I'll go there
again this day.

∽∾

Nevertheless, I want to *see* what Musso and Frank's does look
like inside, considering that it provides a setting in the novel.

So I decide to work a ruse. I head from the brightness of the day into the air-conditioned dimness of Musso and Frank's in late afternoon, immediately to be greeted by a smiling, really old guy—skinny and stoop-shouldered and wearing a dark suit with a dated wide tie, the shirt collar much too big for his bony neck; his voice is faint, a bit shaky even. He holds a stack of large menus in front of him in both arms, the way high school girls used to carry their books, and he asks me if he can direct me to a table.

I look around, try to take it all in, and he looks at me again, saying: "Sir?"

I glance at my watch (a ridiculous thing of translucent lime-green plastic that I bought at a dollar store, which keeps perfect time); I try to project the air that I'm pretty busy, somebody of perhaps consequence who is invariably pretty busy—let's say a movie-business kind of citizen, because deals surely still go down here.

"I was supposed to meet somebody here," I say, looking around some more, "but I guess I'm early."

The guy steps aside, ushering me past him, as he advises that I check this room and also the room next to it. Everything is dark-paneled wood, with the chairs and booths upholstered with red leatherette and the tablecloths bright white, the decor probably unchanged since when West himself reportedly was a regular customer. There are maybe only two or three parties eating, and making a loop through the shadowy place, I already feel a little crummy for giving the line I did to the old guy, who seemed sweet and without question fragile; the middle-aged (and beyond) waiters in their red jackets, unbusy, nod to me, and I walk past the long eating bar in this room—in an alley of sorts, behind a dividing wall—and then past the longer polished-mahogany bar for drinks in the other, nobody sitting at either one of them. Up front by the entrance, the old guy has already announced my plight to the cashier who's fifty or so, a pudgily blond woman with a striking resemblance to the later Shelley Winters and validly part of the time warp herself. At her register she, too, is apparently concerned about my finding the person I'm supposed to meet; she asks me if I checked *both* rooms, to which I answer that I did, and the old guy suggests that maybe I would like to have a drink or a meal and wait.

I tell him no, and that I'm probably way too early and will be back later, adding another overdone concerned glance at the dollar-store plastic watch. Outside again, I stop on the sidewalk, lean against the wall of Musso and Frank's to write, jotting down some details about the interior I just saw—more confirmation.

Going this way and that, the tourists are truly thick now.

Which is when—slipping the notebook and pen into the black Levi's back pocket, about to proceed to the Powerhouse Bar for that envisioned cold Budweiser—I notice something happening on the other side of the Boulevard, farther down and across from the Chinese Theatre, between the old Roosevelt Hotel there that formerly hosted the Oscars and the pillared, buff-stone façade, freshly sandblasted, of the so-called El Capitan Entertainment Center.

I decide to postpone the beer for the moment and head over to see what the commotion is all about.

The crowd on Hollywood Boulevard is always at its *certifiably* thickest right in front of the Chinese Theatre. People do all kinds of things with those imprints in the sidewalk's cement—squatting low to lean over and try to place their own palms in the outlined palms, or standing beside a set of prints for a posed, and paid for, grinning photograph with one of the sizable bunch of twenty-somethings who work their own gig with the tourists, dressed up as Superman or Michael Jackson or—this outfit seems very popular, with at least three girls I see employing it—Catwoman, purring and pawing; however, now some of the crowd appears to have moved across the street, to see for themselves what's going on.

Once Hollywood's Masonic Lodge, the El Capitan Centre (adjoining another restored older building, the El Capitan movie theatre proper, both owned by Disney) is a stately affair, and it houses an auditorium used for TV shows. A young woman in khakis and a blue polo shirt bearing the ABC logo—mile-high cheekbones and full, glossed lips, attractive enough to be a starlet—sits at a small table set up on the sidewalk, trying to give out free tickets to the *Jimmy Kimmel Live* show taping within. There are presently no takers (which anybody who's ever actually watched that decidedly not-funny guy can easily understand), but somebody must have bit for the offer, because apparently a member of the studio audience has had some sort of a medical emergency inside (I hate to say it, but that's what you get for accepting a free Jimmy Kimmel ticket). Already the wailing siren of an EMS unit can be heard, off a ways; still more people drift toward the commotion, blocking the sidewalk, as a panicking bald guy in the very standard tourist's getup of a sport shirt with the tails hanging out and cargo shorts keeps hurrying in and out of the auditorium building, to see if the EMS has, in fact, arrived.

All it takes is the sight of the gleaming scarlet rescue wagon coming this way through the traffic on the Boulevard to draw even more people. The truck swerves over to the curb, the siren ceases its atonal song in a truncated gulp, four muscular young guys in uniforms hop out; the one in charge holds a clipboard, and—the crowd large now—the three others yank from the back of the truck a collapsible stretcher with straps across its white sheet. I watch, stationing myself against a huge pillar of the El Capitan, again taking notes. I write down what those rugged EMS handsomes and their paraphernalia look like (their buzz cuts, their dark blue short-sleeved uniforms, the eerie rattling for the unfolding of the collapsible stretcher on wheels) and also a note to the effect that finally these people marching up and down the Boulevard have found a spectacle: for the crowd something is *happening* at last, even if it is at the expense of somebody else's misfortune and certainly not what they were expecting in just a normal afternoon of sightseeing.

I don't wait for the conclusion. Notebook and pen returned to the back pocket once more, I simply wedge my way out of the pedestrian buildup, repeatedly offering a perfunctory "Excuse me" and trying to smile.

But what transpired there seemed to say something—I find myself thinking about this while enjoying that cold, condensation-dripping brown bottle of Budweiser in the Powerhouse on Highland, where two friendly young guys sitting beside me at the bar and doing shots announce to me right off, for some reason, that they're "Chicano," proud of it and from East L.A., before casually talking about baseball with me as we watch together on ESPN highlights of the previous night's Dodgers game—then I think about it more when I get back to work that evening on the manuscript at the glowing G4 Mac laptop on the desk fringed with cigarette burns in my motel in Chinatown; or, more exactly, it's in the motel, the Royal Pagoda, that it really hits me, as I look up from the computer and right at me staring back from the framed mirror above the desk.

4. Set Aside

Set aside my taking notes in Hollywood, my busily scribbling what I observed regarding locales of scenes in *The Day of the Locust*. That was one thing, but this was another, beyond that, yet related, and for all intents and purposes I actually somehow found myself *in* the climactic scene of the novel, where on the Boulevard a crowd grows out of control in the course of a movie premiere one very frightening night in the 1930s, the big searchlight beams scanning the sky to announce the event (Tod is trampled; Homer kicks to death an obnoxious aspiring child actor who has been taunting him; star-struck, ever-daydreaming Faye maybe looks on at those walking the red carpet, wide-eyed, trying to get a glimpse of still another one of the glamorous actors and actresses stepping out of a limousine to enter the Chinese Theatre). Or, look at it this way: While my crowd scene wasn't the wild and near apocalyptic one of the novel, I did end up in more or less a spookily identical scenario, complete with everyday and probably bored people, a throng in need of—and surely, for many of them, hoping very hard to find—some kind of event in their lives, as said. Why, when I was there the siren wailed loudly, and in the novel, yes, a deafening siren's wail seems to express in that climactic scene—for a broken, half-hysterical Tod, anyway—the utter meaninglessness of just about everything in Hollywood, as encapsulated by the novel's very last lines where Tod starts to madly howl along with it: "The siren began to scream and at first he thought he was making the noise himself.... For some reason this made him laugh and he began to imitate the siren as loud as he could."

Do you see my point?

I mean, I often try to locate the scenes of a novel I love, taking notes, and sometimes use it as a focus in travel, knowing I might write an essay about the book and the place of its setting like the one you're reading now. But taking such notes could be deeper than that, I suspect, well beyond eventually writing any essay, and what is this need that any of us can have to affix to the *unreality* of literature a *reality* it doesn't actually possess? And what does it mean—certainly more tellingly—to feel some ultimate satisfaction that in the *reality* of life (me in Hollywood, finding myself in a climactic crowd scene, one so similar to that in the novel) I proved the true power of the *unreality* of a novel, a product of the imagination and nothing more?

Maybe keep this in mind as I continue, because I think I could be onto something here.

5. That Place Where Literature Does Go to Die, a Second Short Movie

Toward the end of the week, with most of what I feel is good work done on the long manuscript, I realize that I can ease off and do some other things while in the city, before I finish up the trip with a weekend spent by the ocean in Santa

Monica. There are other spots to explore (the old downtown business-and-theater district with its main thoroughfare of South Broadway, rundown yet so wonderfully Latino now you could be in a large, teeming Mexican city, also the cluster of startling new glass-and-steel skyscrapers on the other side of Pershing Square, a textbook on ultra-hip American architecture in itself), and there's an old pal from college, who twenty years earlier was an independent movie producer in L.A., for low-budget slasher and kung fu offerings, actually; following a few extended, laughing phone conversations with him from the motel (those after-all-these-years-and-whatever-happened-to kind of sessions), we've made plans to have dinner.

Plus, there is one more thing to do with respect to West, at the Huntington Library.

✕

A couple of days before I left for L.A.—back in Austin and during my reading around about West—I noticed that there were holdings concerning him at the Huntington. It's the rare books and manuscript library out at what had once been the rich railway magnate's opulent estate in San Marino, a municipality next to Pasadena but even tonier. While I've sometimes flatly expressed my opinion before, in print, that I've never been a big fan of rare books and manuscript libraries, the way that the monetary value attached to their holdings can become more important to some than the literature itself, this time I found myself easing up a little. I thought that while on this quest of rereading and contemplating West as part of the trip, I might go out there and take a look at what they had on him.

But my attempt to obtain a pass for "reader's privileges" to use the library turned complicated. On what should have been routine approval for me as a faculty member at a legitimate university, the person handling registration noticed on the downloaded application I faxed from Austin that I gave no indication of the institution where I received my Ph.D., for which there was a line provided. A series of email exchanges ensued. I explained I was a creative writer in my English department, sans Ph.D., and I got windy (uncharacteristically so, I hope) and informed him outright that I was both a full professor and also somebody holding an endowed named professorship (no big deal, really, but I was trying to get by this guy); strict to the point of being schoolmarmish, he told me that rules were rules, a Ph.D. was *mandatory*, yet he suggested I could solicit two letters of recommendation for an "independent scholar" pass, which is done in the case of somebody not associated with a university, working on the assumption that any university prof is always a Ph.D.— it's also a procedure, I knew, that would take weeks, though I was leaving in a couple of days. I wanted to tell the guy that if he really thought a Ph.D. meant anything when it comes to literature, I might point out to him that historically the bulk of the comment on literature that has, in fact, lasted has been done by actual writers themselves and not scholars (T.S. Eliot on poetry, for instance, not to mention Keats and Shelley and Wallace Stevens; Virginia Woolf, E. M. Forster, Albert Camus, Milan Kundera, etc., on the novel; more specifically, D.H. Lawrence on American literature, Chinua Achebe on *The Heart of Darkness*, or poet Charles Olson in his powerful meditation on *Moby-Dick*, the study *Call Me Ishmael,* which was abandoned as his dissertation for a Harvard Ph.D.—a degree he never finished—and then went on to possibly mark, in its sheer originality and uncanny insight, the most significant of all criticism ever written on that supreme American masterpiece). And I also wanted to tell him that academic criticism lately seldom progresses beyond—to borrow the apt phrasing of eminent University of Virginia scholar Douglas Day—the "earnest drudgery" it sadly is. It's practically a given that with its priggish, soporifically jargonized, perpetual-grad-student prose (did I cover everything in that crabby adjectival list?), such criticism is usually unreadable despite how much extensive research it entails, and because it operates according to whatever trendy critical theory is fashionable at the time, it seems by definition to be programmed to quickly evanesce: just think about how adolescently silly, close to parody, stuff from the 1980s Deconstruction Boom looks today. I guess I really wanted to tell him, or simply invite him, to stop by the old campus building with its dull green linoleum floors and blank yellow plaster walls that houses my own Department of English and step into a classroom, listen in on what gets passed along in lit courses by profs—surely good people, for the most part, but too often nowadays far removed from what's genuinely important in literature (for a lot of them "scholarship" is basically an exercise in asserting personal causes as rigid doctrine—conventional sociology and political science more than anything else— with the whole idea of the transport or even outright magic and mystery of books becoming a rather lost, if not forbidden, concept to espouse on campus today, seen as elitist, while the students themselves seem to *long* for the message of that). In short, I wanted to tell this guy at the library that, everything considered, maybe a Ph.D. was the *last* thing he should be wanting from me.

Nevertheless, up before dawn on the day I was to head out to the Austin airport for my morning flight on Southwest, I thought I might take a chance (i.e., attempt an end run) and email directly the person who was the library's head curator for its literary collections. When I arrived in L.A. a few hours later, I was surprised to find in my inbox a message from that head curator; she informed me that everything had been taken care of—to some extent, anyway. I was being given a very temporary, two-hour access permit to use the library. The guy I originally dealt with emailed me to confirm it (I got the feeling he didn't like me going above his head), and he instructed that I should go online, view the list of the library's West holdings, and pick out *specifically* the documents I would like to see, then email him what they were; the requested materials would be "pulled" and be waiting for me on arrival.

To be honest, I'd started to lose interest in the errand. But seeing that I had a bit of time at the end of the week, and seeing that it had taken much effort to get the clearance, I gave it more consideration. Upon checking, I saw that the L.A. Metro system's brand-new Gold Line—light rail above ground—does go out to Pasadena, so getting to the library wouldn't be too difficult. But maybe what sealed the deal for me was that the schoolmarmish guy said in an email that he would be off work the day I did finally propose for my two-hour visit, and I knew that might make it easy, too, as I was starting to have qualms about my own somewhat noisy dealings with him and probably didn't want to face him personally—after all, he was just doing his job, trying to keep things organized. And, yes, I was feeling good about what I had accomplished on my fiction manuscript, the windows wide open to the balcony walkway of my room at the two-story Royal Pagoda—it looked out to the hill Dodger Stadium sits on, the lights of the ballpark glowing up there like so many clustered little moons this game night—so I *could* put that aside now, granting I hadn't gotten *quite* all done on it that I wanted.

✂

So one evening at the motel I email the schoolmarmish guy, routinely thanking him for all his help. I confirm the proposed time of my visit and say I will have my selections to him pronto.

✂

Actually, I have no real particular materials in mind, and those I eventually do select are offbeat in some cases, but each catches my eye. In the next email I explain that the several items I would like to look at are all in what is listed on the library's Web site as a collection donated by West's biographer Jay Martin—apparently documents he used in his own research. (And I might note here, emphatically, that Martin's biography, the 1974 *Nathanael West: The Art of His Life,* is admirably thorough and engagingly written, a first-rate study. Really try to avoid the newer 2010 biography, *Lonelyhearts* by Marion Meade, which treats West's life alongside that of his wife Eileen McKenney; with its glib tenor announced beforehand by the very subtitle, *The Screw-*

ball World of Nathanael West and Eileen McKenney, the book is thin in pages and large in font, a narrative that often seems cannibalized from other earlier published accounts, as can be the case in too many recent biographies—much of it here is based on Martin, I'd say—and the entire thing presented in a flippant, off-putting voice more fit for a gossipy personal blog than a consideration of a major American writer's life.) Before hitting the send button on the email to the Huntington, I check again that my notation is right: I know that the schoolmarmish guy doesn't fool around and I'm extra careful to give the precise annotation that identifies each item in the online catalogue:

Box 1, folder 5
The Day of the Locust, novel fragment

Box 2, folder 29
Map of L.A., with locations of West's homes marked

Box 2 A, folder 22
Coroner's Report, Imperial County—Photocopy of Jury Inquest on the Death of Nathanael West

Box 2 A, folder 18
"Three Eskimos"

✁

The next day, the Metro ride out to Pasadena is a pleasant half-hour trip—the profuse glass of the car providing large picture windows, the again immaculate train going slow as it first winds out of the old railway-yard tracks of creamy Union Station downtown and then picking up speed through the neighborhoods of houses often precariously tacked onto steep canyon walls (more palms and eucalyptus and blossoming trees of all variety in the honeyed sunshine, vines of red bougainvillea seemingly inundating in spots, swallowing everything whole, and a sky cloudless and blue)—but the two-mile walk from the station to the library in San Marino, in the direction away from the backdrop of the high San Gabriel Mountains in earnest here, isn't so easy. Not caring that I might look goofy in this movie of me—because often when I travel, I somehow seem to be outside myself, watching myself as if in a film—I take from my daypack a mini black rain umbrella, for shade. I realize that the sun from the hours poking around Hollywood and elsewhere in the last few days, despite any promised SPF-50 blockage, has rendered me burnt; it's my hottest day in L.A. yet, at least an even ninety, and for the half hour or so that the walk takes, a straight shot on the sidewalk of residential Allen Avenue, I move along under the impromptu parasol. I pass the groomed homes and apartment complexes of Pasadena, neat to the extreme, and I cross the wide main street of Colorado Boulevard with its restaurants and specialty shops, and I pass a small dignified sign on an iron post indicating the San Marino municipal boundary; up ahead, the impressive black gates of the grounds of the Huntington Library and Museum (a major art collection, of course) finally come into sight.

Nobody else is walking on the long, winding entry drive, bordered by flowers *resplendent* (the only word for it) in churned dark loam, also carefully sculpted shrubbery

on either side. I approach the checkpoint and am met by a
paunchy middle-aged guy wearing a security guard uniform
of shorts and shirt; he steps out of his booth while putting
on a white pith helmet, which assures me that though I've
folded up the little umbrella and stuffed it back into the daypack, the heat is serious and I wasn't as goofy as I thought, to
use it earlier. The Huntington estate comprises the original
huge baroque mansion that's now the art museum—opulent
enough to rival anything in regal Europe, giving solid tes-
tament to what might be seen as the indulgence, and associated futile vanity, of having altogether too much money for
one's own good in this brief life—and the library building,
as huge and itself probably more Georgian in architectural
style, along with several assorted lesser structures (a domed
ornamental temple and such); the entire enterprise is set in
two hundred acres of a sprawling, park-like expanse of ponds
and tufted lawns and extensive "botanical gardens." Having
found my name on his printout of an official visitors' list for
the day, the guard in the pith helmet smilingly decides that
I've walked far enough in the heat already, and he says he
will use his canopied golf cart to take me the rest of the way,
deliver me right to the library's steps. As we hum along the
winding drive in the cart, there's small talk about where I'm
from—"Texas," I tell him, then add, "but originally from
Rhode Island," something I always point out even if I have
lived in Austin for thirty years, the guy liking the essential
idea of a state being as altogether far away as *Rhode Island*—
and he next asks me where I am staying in L.A.—"Chinatown," I tell him, and he likes the idea of that, too, definitely: "Now that's part of the *real* Los Angeles," he assures me.
I suppose I now appreciate the convoluted route it took to

arrive here—through such vivid canyon terrain on the train, then walking alone down empty and oddly immaculate suburban streets in the heat under an umbrella, to be met by a stranger in a pith helmet who at last ushers me to my destination, an elongated, looming classical edifice maybe perfectly suited for a mysterious Paul Delvaux canvas—and there is the sense of a *journey* to it, something of a dream, maybe.

I find the office of the schoolmarmish guy's assistant, named Juan and as friendly as the security guard. He has me sign some papers I don't bother to read, then gives me a giant yellow Ticonderoga pencil with thick blunt lead and a virgin-pink eraser, what could be a parody of a pencil, and tells me only notes in pencil are allowed, which is common procedure in such libraries, I know. He escorts me to a small room with lockers, for storage of my daypack, and directs me toward the reading room. There, I am handed a printed sticky-back nametag by the serious, whispering woman staffing the counter, who tells me I must wear the tag at all times (it clearly states: "*Non-Renewable*"). I choose a table, getting down to making the most out of my two-hour window of opportunity.

I've been in rare books and manuscript libraries like this before—here little glowing lamps on the long light-mahogany tables, where the scattering of researchers read or click away on keyboards, green carpeting for the room in this case and tasteful beige walls. Along the shelves around the periphery are the usual busts of luminaries: the bronze casts in the Huntington offer a dramatis personae ranging from Aristotle to Shakespeare to, maybe not so predictably, John Paul Jones. Big toy-like pencil on the table, my pocket notebook open and ready, I start going through the folders, manila with gray ribbon ties, taking out the artifacts one by one and soon completely immersed in how interesting they are. I start with what should be the most routine of them, the map, telling myself I will work my way up to that one folder with some manuscript pages of the very novel I have been ruminating on—thinking and thinking about it here in L.A.—*The Day of the Locust*; actually, once I get going, I have no idea where I really am, the stuff is so *damn* interesting.

I open the folder marked neatly on the tab label, **Box 2, folder 29: Map of L.A.**, showing the locations of West's various residences; it's a 1967 common Mobil street map for the City of Los Angeles with the long-gone red Pegasus logo adorning the cover, the kind they used to give out for free at gas stations and once called "glove-compartment maps"; I spread it out; I know this is what Jay Martin must have used in his biographical research; there are ovals scrawled in ball-point around several street names, a half dozen or more of them, and I locate Ivar Street, then write down a note about the other streets marked; a few are in the swank hills above Hollywood, as West (a bachelor with his hunting dogs) did go to live in rented houses there when his screenwriting career became solid; I fold up the map, concentrating and figuring which flap goes where, the way you do with an accordionized map, and slip it back in the manila folder, put it aside. I pick up the next folder in the stack**, Box 2 A, folder 18: "Three Eskimos,"** carefully remove the several sheets of yellowing loose-leaf, the lines of it black rather than the usual light blue; in West's own handwriting, dark pencil, is the manuscript of a short story unpublished in his lifetime but later included in the Library of America definitive edition of his collected works; I like looking at West's handwriting itself, oversized and boxy, for this satiric tale about a family of Eskimos brought to Hollywood from Alaska as extras for a movie, and I write in my notebook that this same family becomes the Gingo Eskimo Family, who in *The Day of the Locust* are friends of Faye Greener's vaudevillian father and have decided they like Hollywood life, refusing to return to Alaska and surviving on raw fish bought from Jewish delicatessens; I am especially careful with these pages, dry and fragile, and after I skim through the story I put the sheets back in that folder, placing it on the folder with the map. I pick up the third folder, **Box 2 A, folder 22: Coroner's Report, Imperial County—Photocopy of Jury Inquest on the Death of Nathanael West**, and I lift out the dozen or so elongated legal pages, beginning with pre-printed boilerplate where blanks are filled in with the names of the judge and inquest jury involved in this investigation into West's accident and then offering the typed transcript proper as recorded by a court reporter, like a play's format, and quite frank and detailed when it comes to the question if West had been drinking (empty Mexicali Beer bottles were found in the wreckage, a state trooper testifies, though he concedes they could have been consumed at any time well before the accident, left bouncing around in the wood-paneled station wagon); that's followed by even more uncomfortable exchanges indeed, such as one that's indicative of a whole other sorry era in America, let's hope—there's the particularly awkward moment when the driver of the other car, a family man, testifies, and then one of the jurors (in what I hear as a slow, bigoted country voice) has an additional question for the trooper, with the Deputy D.A. coming in after that, regarding the matter of who *exactly* West was:

JUROR: Is West a Spanish or American boy?

OFFICER TILLMAN: Evidently American.

DEPUTY D.A. FREEMAN *(perhaps exasperated with a question like that*—my insert*)*: He and his wife lived in North Hollywood, didn't they?

I write down some notes, including the dialogue lines from the transcript that you've just read here in this movie of me, and I put the stapled-together photocopy of the report back into the folder and place it on top of the two others I've already been through.

I had only a roll and coffee for lunch, and all the walking, those couple of miles in the sun earlier, is starting to catch up with me. I'm getting tired in the library (I look around—a prim elderly woman working at her laptop next to me smiles; I see a young guy a few tables over examining manuscripts and wearing a baggy sweatshirt and a black knit cap that says "Berlin" on the side, and I like the fact he doesn't seem, well, scholarly), as I do finally get to that last folder, the one I have in a way been saving, **Box 1, folder 5: The Day of the Locust, novel fragment**; before long I'm completely lost, and then some, in the less than a dozen pages of faint typescript on crisp onionskin, and, as it turns out, I go way beyond my 1:30-3:30 begrudgingly issued time slot (however, now here, I doubt anybody cares about any of that, and I suspect it wouldn't even bother the schoolmarmish guy of the rules-are-rules mindset if he was around and this wasn't his day off); for me, to actually see West at work, with his penciled-in word changes and in two cases complete typewritten rewrites of pages, proves the very best thing of all in the Huntington; sometimes it's just a small alteration that results in large difference, and at one point I write in my notebook how it constitutes a master stroke, the way West in the manuscript originally introduces Tod Hackett as a personage who would become famous for his well-known painting "The Burning of Los Angeles" then changes that to Tod Hackett who is simply working on a painting of that title, as he is in the published novel (the former would have been trite, making Tod subsequently famous like that, not the right oblique touch whatsoever); at another point I write in my notebook that I am now seeing up close the composition of some of the earliest pages in the novel, where Tod, at the end of his work day, walks leisurely from his movie studio to where he lives at the San Bernardino Arms, and I also write down that I myself followed the same walk described in those pages the day I was first out in Hollywood, retracing his steps from the studio that used to be Columbia and then up the hill of Ivar Street to the Pa-Va-Sed Apartments (odd that the pages of this brief manuscript "fragment" should contain that exact scene—another mirror mirroring?); I linger over the manuscript pages, eventually finish.

I look around the room again before packing everything up for return to the front desk, the same serious woman there, nodding but not smiling. I tug on the light suit jacket I brought with me to wear with the black Levi's and another open-collared dress shirt, perhaps to appear presentable in these surroundings. I'm really tired, and I tell myself that as very interesting as the afternoon has been, I do know what I've always known—that never mind the off-putting practice of collecting literary artifacts as pricey possessions, it's true that the *whole concept* of a rare books and manuscript library, with so many scholars busily working away—the never-ending routine of research and by-the-numbers academic critical analysis, more often than not mere fuel for the promotion-and-tenure machine—really has little to do with the rhapsodic transport of the literature itself, read by the amazed reader himself or herself, ultimately excited; when all is said and done, a room like this undeniably is what it is: *a place where literature goes to die.*

After leaving the library, I make an attempt at wandering around the grounds of the Huntington beyond the library building, in back where the art museum and those touted, supposedly renowned botanical gardens are, but the project is pretty short-lived: I am suddenly *absolutely* tired at the end of this long day (the nametag still stuck on my shirt elicited a nod from an attendant and then her waving me through the turnstile, gratis, at the little colonnade concourse for tickets, twelve bucks otherwise), and I don't even muster the energy to go into the museum to see any of the paintings.

I know that with my trip just about over I look forward to dinner with my old college pal that evening (truth of the matter is that I'm both tired and even a touch depressed, which can happen toward the end of a trip, the realization that "Now this is over, what the hell do I do next in my life?" and I am already thinking again of what I came here to get away from, the sadness of my friend's illness back in Austin—because to have a debilitating stroke at just fifty is colossally unfair—and also the absurdity of the departmental politics I foolishly let myself get roped into at the end of the semester), yes, I look forward to meeting up with the pal from college, a guy with little interest in books—sometimes I have to take a break, I know, from literature and its trappings, wondering too much about books and letting that eat up my life.

But my afternoon in the Huntington Library does have something to do with what happened to me that other afternoon up in Hollywood, when I seemed to not only track down more of the settings of *The Day of the Locust* but also walk right into a scene from the novel, diligently taking notes about it all the while as well.

And if I've served up two short movies of me here, there's still a transcendent—or maybe metaphysical—trailer of sorts to come, an attempt to bring everything here together, after a belated brief "intermission" with my college pal. (I really hope I'm not sounding altogether too hokey with this movie motif—and there is the excuse that I *am* in L.A.) I leave San Marino.

I ride the Gold Line light-rail train back to Chinatown.

6. Time and the Sneaky Way It Somehow Passes

My college pal, despite the fact he currently lives in Westwood, knows Chinatown well. After finishing law school in Los Angeles years before, he worked for the city's legal aid program, downtown, often going to one of the dozens of restaurants to choose from within those several self-contained blocks that make up Chinatown, the neighborhood's trademark pagoda rooflines everywhere (like the roofline outlined in red neon at night of my funky Royal Pagoda Motel where I've been so comfortable, an establishment that proudly advertises, "Built in 1964 and a hotspot for Asian celebrities of the era," among them, as boasted, "Apasra Hongsakula—Ms. [sic] Universe 1965"). On the phone he tells me he'll be there by seven, his voice gentle and even-toned:

"No, you just wait for me at your motel, Pete, relax after your long day, rest for a while. And I'll try to relax, too, in the traffic, get on the freeway with some music playing and be there in less than an hour. I'm really up for some awesome Chinese food."

After he navigates me on the walk through the back streets of Chinatown, we sit wielding chopsticks at the restaurant—one he remembers as his favorite for seafood when working legal aid, an inexpensive place where I have possibly the best scallops in stir-fried crisp vegetables anybody could ever long for—and we *are* relaxed. We talk more about old friends, laugh, and we do an awful lot of filling in on what has happened to us in life, successes and failures, not only on what passes for the career front but also in experiences with women, both of us on our own again at this stage, admittedly rather old to be "dating"—but both of us *do* date, albeit awkwardly at our age, have a lot of fun with it, and we laugh about that. Athletically tall, buff from working out in the gym—something obvious, with him wearing a tight, bright yellow T-shirt, complete with a thin gold necklace, L.A.-ish—he's a good-looking guy; his hair is still dark and cut short, and most of all it is his very white smile that shows that while both of us qualify for all that AARP stuff embarrassingly clogging the mailbox, he now and then seems entirely the same guy I knew in college. He was a great skier back then and on the university's varsity team, after that a full-time member of a ski manufacturer's sponsored promotional team before law school, an acknowledged innovator in "hot-dog skiing" when the sport was just being invented. He's proud of his two grown children, whom he raised largely on his own after his marriage didn't work out, balancing that with some law work conducted out of his office at home and, more so, business deals; he tells me that with a recently acquired degree in finance, his twenty-two-year-old daughter ("bright as all hell") is living with him in the house in Westwood at the moment and working in L.A., while she waits to start a job she's excited about on Wall Street in the fall.

Having not seen him in years, since right after graduation, to be exact, I've heard from other college friends that for a while his business ventures included movies, an independent producer with a small production company for low-budget films. I ask him about it now and he explains it was all modest and *very* low budget—the slasher and American kung fu movies—though there was opportunity with such in the late eighties and early nineties. With a cameo from a recognizable actor booked cheaply—Lee Marvin, one time—he could sell a package for good distribution and see a decent return on the investment, Sony involved at least once. Still, in the end he was glad he got out of it, noting: "The whole movie thing is all sleaze—not that I wasn't doing my part."

I laugh, and he asks me how I, a short story writer and novelist, never got caught up in the movie thing myself. I tell him I've probably always been too impractical, perhaps naive; also, I grew up in a house where books were what mattered (before marriage my mother was a school librarian) and I lived in a semi-rural area and didn't even go to movies much as a kid, to develop any early hunger to get involved in them. But I go on to explain there was that one occasion, what I've told people about before to get a laugh.

After the appearance of a novel of mine years ago, I was approached by a producer who liked the book and my work overall; he asked me to write an original treatment for development, hopefully, into a full-fledged screenplay. The producer was Ronnie Shedlo (he died recently, not all that old), who had a reputation of being an honorable maverick in Hollywood and was involved in some good work (he did the film *Back Roads* with Sally Field and Tommy Lee Jones, the latter at Harvard with my pal and me in the late sixties, Tommy Lee characteristically leathery and gravelly voiced even then as an undergrad, when I'd encounter him in the teacup of Sever Lecture Hall for the full year of Chaucer that was required of all honors English majors at the time; I also later learned—weird, too, in the context of what I'm writing here—that Shedlo was the original producer who put together the package for the fine 1975 film of *The Day of the Locust* directed by John Schlesinger, which had Karen Black with bleached golden hair set in a shimmering Marcel wave as a convincing Faye Greener and Donald Sutherland, hauntingly blank-faced, as a perfect Homer Simpson, yet accounts indicate that Shedlo withdrew from the final project when pressure from others who were part of it demanded certain casting or perhaps even asked for textual compromise, maybe on the script written by Waldo Salt of *Midnight Cowboy* notoriety). I tell my pal now that at first I didn't take it seriously whatsoever, saw it as but a dreamy long shot that might mean some easy money, and when I sent Shedlo a fifteen-page treatment I whipped up quickly, replete with every cliché you'd find in any Clint Eastwood tough-guy-cop performance, Shedlo bluntly told me on the phone—calling from his own home in Beverly Hills, no less—that if he wanted crap like that he never would have approached me to begin with and could have found a million people there in L.A. to give it to him. Two things resulted: first, an amazement from literary-snooty me that a Hollywood producer had read so much, knew literature inside out, I soon learned, and, secondly, once we did move toward a screenplay, based on a subsequent, much better treatment I gave him, I realized that while a treatment was like a short story and easy for me, I was no good at delivering a finished working script—it's *hard* to get dialogue in a script to both sound natural and carry the machinations of plot, taking a skill that I, for one, didn't possess, am still sort of intimidated by, actually.

"So nothing came of it?" my college pal asks me.

"No, it all got more absurd. As Shedlo started to talk about points, what my cut would be according to a contract if the thing ever were made and that kind of financial stuff, and with him about to fly to Texas to work on the script with me, well, at that stage my publisher—or maybe the film agent I had then, because there was a Hollywood agent who represented me through the publisher—in any case, somebody got word that there was big-time interest with real big-time money on another front for movie rights, coming from a group of secretive investors who were apparently crazy about my novel and its somewhat *noir* portrait of decadent life in the fast lane of booming urban Texas in the 1980s."

I tell him I was advised to let the Ronnie Shedlo project go, which I did, and wait for the new people to make a move, as the secretive investors turned out to be a bunch of, indeed, pretty big-time drug dealers in Dallas, represented in their business ventures by a lawyer named—could it get any better?—*Robin Hood*, who had approached my publisher—nothing but bothing ever coming of that.

He laughs.

"Movies," he says, the twin batons of bamboo chopsticks poised in his crossed fingers, smiling that white smile, shaking his head.

Walking back to my motel, where he has parked the sleek black BMW coupe that seems to embarrass him some, there is a full moon in the inky blue night sky over empty Chinatown, with its pull-down steel shutters on shop fronts padlocked tight, the silhouettes of those horned pagoda rooflines all around us, and we both agree how much we'd enjoyed ourselves and we shouldn't let so much time slip away between get-togethers like this.

There in the parking lot, after more talk while we stand around—continued remembering of guys we knew from playing on sports teams and such back in college, wonderful old girlfriends back in college as well—he finally opens the BMW door there in the moonlight and is about to get into that beige-leather cockpit, the car new enough that the inside still smells like a luggage store. Soft-voiced, he tells me something along the lines of:

"You know, I look in the mirror, Pete, I see me, and I say to myself—who the hell is that guy? I mean, I don't feel *that* old."

I try to assure him he doesn't look very old, which he doesn't.

7. The Transcendent Trailer

OK, here goes, and let me see if I can at last put some of this together, because I *have* been thinking more and more about much of this, now that I am back in Austin.

I am wondering about what seemed to be at the heart of those two movies of me there in L.A. during that week or

so and if it does reveal that something bigger I've been trying to get at for a long time now, including well before this
trip, something essentially metaphysical. I would like to say
that it all fell whisperingly into place when I was confronted
with those near symbols of the metaphysical, locales that in
themselves cause you to just gaze and gaze and feel that cru-
cial insight is imminent, you are about to finally *understand*
(for instance, looking out at, mesmerizingly so and alone, the
immense blue Pacific early one morning while walking on
deserted Santa Monica Beach, with its bright white sands and
clusters of palms, during the trip's last couple of days I spend
out there; or looking down at, equally mesmerizingly so and
alone, the vast American desert from a plane, and there are
the erosion-clawed chocolate mountains, the ongoing, seemingly endless orange sand flats, as seen from 30,000 feet up
on my afternoon Southwest return flight, where the cabin is
close to empty and I have the row of seats to myself, the en-
gines droning on and on), sure, it would be somehow perfect
if I could say it all came together for me at a moment such
as one of those. But it didn't. And even now as I sit writing
this on a July morning in the back bedroom of my apartment
at 1407 West 39th ½ Street and with the air conditioning
laboring away here in Austin, where I've signed on again to
teach every afternoon in a five-week summer session because
of some hefty bills that really have to be taken care of, I can
only try—but I will try—to piece it together. And if it is to be
approached in terms of the transcendent, I might go right to
the top and summon a quote from the literary master of matters transcendent and metaphysical, of course, Borges himself,
who once pronounced: "We accept reality so readily perhaps
because we suspect that nothing is real."

True, in the past dozen years I have been doing a lot of exactly what I did out in L.A., traveling to a place where a document of literature I love is set and rereading the book there, to see what happens. (Other trips have taken me to Buenos Aires and rereading Borges there, to Paris and rereading the French surrealists there, to Oxford, Mississippi, and rereading Faulkner there, to Cuernavaca and rereading Malcolm Lowry there, to Tunis and rereading Flaubert— specifically his *Salammbô,* about ancient Carthage—there.) While the time in Los Angeles was really about an attempt to clear my head out for a bit, get away from problems that had been closing in on me in my own shaky life in Austin and work on revising the long fiction manuscript, no distractions, I think that in the end there was an equal measure of this ongoing pursuit, too, the rereading of West there, contemplating *The Day of the Locust.* Still, what does taking all those notes mean, as I seek out the places in a writer's work, this obsession I have—or any of us has—to do that sort of thing? And what does going to a library to look at an author's actual manuscripts mean, touch what he or she has touched, see firsthand the machinations of the airy imagination as it composes and rephrases with cross-outs and inserts right there on the page? And does it indicate that in the consummate Borgesian inversion, paradox within paradox, we suspect the unreality of reality, while we also have a strong desire to affix some reality to unreality, as I suggested earlier? Which is to say, I confirmed in the world the place—that apartment house—where West's conjured-up characters lived, and I confirmed in the world the supposed fictional happenings in the book with my somehow walking along Hollywood Boulevard and finding myself in that screwed-up scene of a pantingly blank crowd hungry for some definition of themselves in their own lives—either by proximity to celebrity or in this case the outright calamity of somebody else—something to give a measure of meaning, in fact, to themselves and their own presence on Hollywood Boulevard right then that sunny afternoon...and I...and...

8. . . .

(...and...and I...and I embarked on what seems like some dream journey out to a millionaire's residence in a vast verdant park, evidence in itself of the fleetingness of the materialistic, to sit in a lamplit reading room and examine the yellowing few pages of fading type on onionskin for those revisions of The Day of the Locust—a guy at another table with a knit cap that said "Berlin" staring back at me every once in a while, now that I think of it, strangely dreamlike, too—and there was my folding up so carefully, so silently, a map, one flap over another over another of the thing, trying not to make any noise that might disturb anybody else working at the light-mahogany tables in the quiet library, that old 1967 Mobil map with the spots circled where West had once actually lived, Nathanael West whose work was painfully neglected during his own lifetime and who was killed much too young, and...and...)

9. . . . continued

(...and West was somebody who did conjure up with the magic of words, simple little black marks on a white pulp page, such beautifully crafted documents, two lasting novels that tell us of some of the biggest secrets of all in our lives, probe the essence of the underlying concept of a forever-dreaming America, too, and add to that the fact that The Day of the Locust is about Hollywood, where unreality is the defining reality of the place, because throughout the novel West

plays with this premise, his main character Tod walks through the studio back lot with its false-front sets for Wild West towns and Manhattan neighborhoods, and there's one scene where the re-creation of the Battle of Waterloo for a big-budget movie results in a flimsy back-lot set, constructed to resemble a hill, collapsing under the marching boots and pounding horse hooves of Wellington's troops, and with that disaster the battle that determined a large part of the history of the Western World turns out altogether differently, altered by the imagination and somehow almost changing the entire course of history itself as facilely as that, as whimsically as that, while during the whole episode a somewhat crazed God-like director futilely keeps giving stage directions through his megaphone amid the hopeless total confusion—sure, add that, a note about history itself, which is time, even add what that in turn suggests, the element of the central elusive spookiness of time, above all, and there is my college pal forever standing in the moonlight of the little courtyard parking lot of the Royal Pagoda Motel beside his sleek black BMW wondering how he got so old, having no sense of it, he softly confesses, time as unreal yet real as anything else, and I…and I…and…)

10. Nowhere

No, admittedly I'm getting nowhere, even as I find myself slipping into pseudo-Faulknerian parenthetical riffs on my Mac keyboard, almost a vaguely subconscious level and sort of a rapid, imagistic free-falling that's pleasant enough (man, did you just see that happening? and what's there above is pretty much undoctored, honestly, except to insert the italics, plus the numbers and evasive headings), but if nothing else, I have brought up what could be the telling conundrum, and when it comes to the purpose of a trailer (here's a good dodge, and again excuse my running the risk of wearing *very* thin with use of these movie metaphors), it's always supplied to give you just a glimpse, I'd say. There's never the whole thing—a trailer merely gets you interested, and *thinking*.

11. Thinking

Thinking the way you *do* when you look down while flying at a never-ending desert in the stillness of a sun-struck afternoon, thinking the way you also *do* when on a beach alone and you silently gaze at the wide blueness of the ocean itself, tucked in by distant mountains on either side, with the level line of the horizon marred only by a white cruise ship, its cabins stacked high, heading to a destination surely unknown—that sense of your experiencing a major realization, but, on the brink of it, never quite there with that something you *seem* to already know.

12. "Why Write Novels?"—As West Asked

Or, look at it another way, and here is at least one thing I definitely know, a final point that's hopefully trumping, for a solution: Why be crazy enough to write novels or embark on any work that aspires to be—and it takes a measure of daring to say this, seeing that it's all but forbidden in English departments as well as plenty of other places nowadays—serious art?

I'll tell you why, and maybe this is *it*—because art itself, in any of its many variations and permutations, is one way of at least attempting to repeatedly convince ourselves that the illusory stay on this planet *is* something, that life is worthily and ultimately, though often heartbreakingly, wonderful, granting it does slip away altogether too fast—writing a novel does, in the end, let the novelist and readers believe at last the most absurd proposition and craziest premise of all: *We are here.*

13. Even

You know, even the schoolmarmish, rules-are-rules guy at the Huntington, who I never as much as saw or actually spoke to in our exchange of emails, never heard his voice, is here in this world, bless him, and I've proved it beyond any doubt he or anybody else might have just by my own writing about him. Also, don't forget that wannabe songwriter, the overweight guy with a ponytail there on Hollywood Boulevard one very hot day in late May of 2010 dreaming of his "Hey, Lardass!" number being recorded, becoming a monster hit, and I've surely proved it when it comes to him, too, the lovable poor bastard.

2012, FROM *MEMOIR JOURNAL*

WALKING: ANOTHER ESSAY ON WRITING

1. Roller Luggage

Both times it had to do with walking, and both in what you might call "other places." Not so oddly, I guess. In Paris I had been walking for about a half hour already that Sunday afternoon.

I had no real agenda, other than getting out of my apartment in the Marais for a while in the good weather, heading up toward the Place de l'Opéra and the streets behind it with the big department stores. I wanted to see if I could maybe determine where the old Café Certa had been, the spot that figures prominently in what has to be one of the neglected masterpieces of French Surrealism, Louis Aragon's *Paris Peasant*. I was in Paris for a semester, teaching again at a university there, and at the moment I was immersing myself in a personal project of reading as much as I could Surrealist prose, which overall tends to get sold short at the expense of the movement's poetry.

I had logged enough long walks around the city already that I knew it was wise to always have a mini umbrella poked into the pocket of my zip-up jacket—in Paris in autumn the weather can often change, dramatically and fast. But this day the sky was so big and blue over the stately buff-stone buildings lining the empty thoroughfare of Boulevard de Magenta, the plane trees showing leaves as fiery as anything in New England, that I soon realized I definitely wouldn't need it. I probably also realized, or assured myself, that wearing the springy, and basic, black-and-white nylon Reeboks had been a good idea, the essential bounce of them, even if they did look a little goofy. Actually, continuing along, I tugged off the jacket and carried it under my arm, eventually deciding the day wasn't *quite* warm enough for that, and when I did put it back on, I spotted the Gare du Nord. Which is when I think it started.

I hadn't been in the Gare du Nord for a while, so I thought it might be worth taking a swing through it now on this walk. I headed that way.

There was the cluster of cafés and hotels surrounding the station and then the façade of the impressive edifice itself. A central fan window rose almost the height of it, with sculpted toga-clad personages atop the entrance's long row of heavy swinging doors. (While walking, I suppose that I was thinking of the woman I had been seeing before I came to France. I suppose I was thinking some about my classes, too, there in the university's stark classroom building over by the Panthéon, the Sorbonne Nouvelle and a different university than the one in Paris where I had been a visiting faculty member years before; I had to teach only once a week, on Fridays. One class was in creative writing, this time delivered in English to sweet, hopeful first-year Anglo-American Studies students whose English really wasn't very good and who probably weren't ready for creative writing even in their own language; the other was in the theater department, a class on Tennessee Williams, where the equally sweet and hopeful students, budding actors and actresses, had next to no English for the most part and I often had to resort to conversing in French, despite the departmental powers that be repeatedly telling me that the whole idea was to stay tough and give them only English.) The concourse of the Gare du Nord within stretched enormous, a wide polished floor and the bright afternoon light coming through the lofty glass-and-cast-iron roof providing a pleasant glare to it all, like sunshine on a frozen pond, maybe; automated signs clickingly shuffled arrival and departure information. At the dead-ends of the platform tracks were the sleek, streamlined snouts of the high-speed TGV locomotives repeated one after another, massive silver machines, about a half dozen of them in a line facing that main lobby with its newsstands and coffee counters. And gathered before one locomotive, in the glare and amid a spread-out clutter of all sorts of bags and bulky suitcases, was a pack of young women, chicly dressed and very blond; they were chatting and laughing, occasionally looking up to the schedule announcements above. I told myself they must have been Dutch or Scandinavian—all strikingly blond like that, nearly uniformly so—and, of course, the Gare du Nord does serve northern European destinations.

As I said, it *started* then, but I wasn't sure of it yet.

Farther on, it was admittedly strange to be walking through the pocket with the famous Parisian department stores, true Belle Époque landmarks, and seeing the streets thoroughly deserted. I passed the window displays and their many mirrors that tossed back moving images of me, and I even poked around the alleys behind the stores and the scruffy loading docks; it was cooler there in the shadows, but once out in the sun again, walking on the comfortable Reeboks, it became warm again, though not quite as much so now as an hour before when I'd first set out.

Louis Aragon's 1926 *Paris Peasant* is a long personal essay, much like a journal, about the author's life and metaphysical imaginings at twenty-five. In the book, the Café Certa serves as the central meeting place for the group of then relatively unknown young writers and painters who are his close friends, an iconoclastic coterie that began with Dada interests and would eventually be celebrated worldwide as a bona fide movement, the Surrealists. The café also becomes for Aragon, when alone, a good nook for writing. There he works on his poems and essays. He rubs elbows with the habitués from the neighborhood, soon backing their struggle to try to keep the vintage shopping arcade that houses the Certa from being demolished in the name of progress, before it belatedly falls prey to Baron Haussmann's controversial master plan to rehab Paris that lingered well into the twentieth century. Why, at one point in *Paris Peasant,* Aragon goes as far as reproducing on the page, as part of the text, an exact facsimile of the café's cocktail menu, a "Tarif des Consommations," ranging from (untranslated) the "Kiss Me Quick" and the "Pick Me Hup" and the "Sherry Cobler" (one *b*) to what seems to be the very special, and undoubtedly extremely dangerous, "Pêle-Mêle Mixture" (*prix 2 F.50*).

But walking now, it was tough for me to get a bead on exactly where the Café Certa had been, there in the vicinity of the big, open plaza in front of yet another of those full six train stations in Paris, this time the Gare Saint-Lazare. On the city's western side, it serves the lines going to and coming from the U.K., via the old pre-tunnel ferry connection, and I told myself that the Certa's menu with its endearing English might have been practical rather than affected when considered in that light, seeing that some of its customers would have been British. However, looking around, going up and down streets between the station and the Boulevard des Italiens, I knew that much had certainly changed, and I realized that many of the buildings were completely different now and sometimes also renumbered, so that for me it wouldn't be, after all, a matter of at least seeing where the café had *once* been.

I had looked up the address for the current Café Certa in the *Bottin*, the hefty Paris phone book, before I left my apartment, and it matched the information that Aragon himself had provided back in 1926. In a footnote he explains that at the time of his completing *Paris Peasant* the Café Certa was already gone, moved to a "new location" on Rue d'Isly and "near the old London Bar," though he makes no mention of going there anymore. And on the other side of the station, deep in a nest of more Sunday-empty side streets, I did find the Rue d'Isly and I did see the current Certa. I would have gone in for a coffee, but for me the place looked too neat today, even after so many years of operation in this location— too upscale. There was a pricey dinner menu in the front window, and on the other side of the glass waiters in proper black trousers and crisp white shirts were preparing tables for

what might have been the evening's well-heeled dinner clientele—I understood why Aragon himself had perhaps kept
his distance.

And still walking, starting to head back, I knew I was
appreciative of the fact that attempting to locate the Café
Certa had, if nothing else, given me a destination, a vague
reason to get out of my apartment on such a fine October
afternoon, to just walk and walk like this. (I possibly thought
some more about my classes, thought, too, much more about
the woman I had been seeing back home and who had become, well, dear to me.) I looked at my watch, saw that the
time it gave was exactly the same as that on the clock atop
the Gare Saint-Lazare. I figured I would work my way back
to the Marais along the Grands Boulevards, and there would
be plenty of cafés en route to choose from if I wanted to take
a bit of a rest—which was when it started again.

Or, more so, when it *happened*.

I waited for the light to turn at sort of a traffic semicircle—
devoid of any traffic, it faced the plaza in front of the station,
with Gare Saint-Lazare as impressive as Gare du Nord even
without the latter's ornate carved statuary—and I saw what I
maybe hadn't noticed when I had been looking around there
only a half hour before. I saw how from all sides of the traffic
semicircle people on foot seemed to be converging on the
station, not a crowd, but people approaching the station—
singly or sometimes in couples—from all directions. It was
the end of a weekend, a Sunday with the sunshine beginning
to soften and taking on a thick, honeyish hue that made the
recently sandblasted Gare Saint-Lazare more golden than it
was, also made the colors of the clothing of the people converging on the station from the empty streets—moving in a

diminishing fan toward it and then across the paved plaza—yes, those colors more true than they were, too, a red jacket here, a very royal blue one there. Many of them were pulling roller luggage, walking along with suitcases on little wheels with quiet reservation, expressionless, as if it were just so much work they had to do. Everybody returning.

I stared at it all.

I don't know what it was. It would be easy to say it was a combination of understandably intriguing imagery—travelers at the end of a weekend heading home, not only the lovely contingent of blond young women in the Gare du Nord standing around in front of the long-snouted futuristic locomotives, a scene that was pretty wondrous in itself, but travelers from everywhere seeming to have materialized from all the deserted streets of Paris now. And there was that clock high on the station's topmost gable at the head of the sloping plaza, its sizable Roman numerals and tapering hands, black on white, telling them they had trains to catch, weary as they were, they had eventual destinations somewhere in what would surely be the dark night of a station platform in some distant town or other faraway city—it would be very easy indeed to give the whole thing a somewhat logical explanation like that.

But the truth of the matter, and what I honestly still remember to this day, is that I didn't want to explain it, there was nothing to be interpreted. And what I know is that it simply left me with an undeniable feeling, not about the scene in particular then or wanting to later depict or write about it, but just a feeling, strong and sure and almost dizzying in my longing, an overwhelming and tangible need.

I really felt like I wanted to be writing my own fiction, like nothing else in the world, to pick up where I had left off earlier that morning on the short story I had been working on. I really felt that I just wanted to be there again at the desk, writing that short story, or anything else, for that matter.

The traffic light changed. I crossed the street and headed toward the Place de l'Opéra and the Grands Boulevards. I didn't stop for a coffee in the course of the long walk back, and I just desired, very much so, to be in the apartment in the Marais, *writing again.*

2. The Statue of Chopin by the Sea

This time I was in Brazil, Rio de Janeiro specifically.

You see, lately I have been doing something, as I've written about before. I go to a place where literature I love is set, and the travel doesn't entail any other express purpose, like that of the teaching appointment I had been lucky enough to land in Paris—this kind of travel is always altogether different. What I do is pack a small bag with a few changes of clothes and a few texts, and I head off for a couple of weeks, solo, to reread a writer there, immersing myself in the work "on the premises." True, I've read Borges stories in Buenos Aires, and I've read Flaubert's meditation on ancient Carthage, the novel *Salammbô*, in Tunisia. I've read Faulkner in Oxford, Mississippi, holed up in a great little twenty-five-buck-a-night motel called the Ole Miss right off the main square with its antebellum white courthouse there, and I've read what could be ensconced among the handful of my absolutely favorite modern novels, Malcolm Lowry's *Under the Volcano,* in Cuernavaca.

And in Brazil it was Machado de Assis's 1881 *Epitaph of a Small Winner.* The novel recounts the odd life of an elegant

Rio gentleman, Brás Cubas, and is presented in the form of an autobiography written from the other side of the grave; actually, the spooky narrative strategy gets announced right up front by an alternate, but not as good, English translation from the Portuguese that sticks to the original title, *The Posthumous Memoirs of Brás Cubas*. Machado's book is essentially an experimental one that was far ahead of its time, a text that became important to a lot of the generation of daring American writers who made their mark in the 1960s and '70s—everybody from John Barth to Donald Barthelme to Susan Sontag, it seems—and I guess it took hold in my writer's psyche about that time, too. The power lies in the sheer virtuosity of the performance, a tour de force both in its nervous, darkly humorous take on life, with a postmodern (Beckettian?) mindset well before even modernism, and an unflagging commitment to startling invention in style and structure throughout.

And after over a week in the city, rereading Machado, exploring some of the Rio associated with him (where he had lived; his burial crypt built into a hillside in São João Batista cemetery; the forgotten little museum room of manuscripts and artifacts from his life tucked upstairs in the Brazilian Academy of Letters building downtown, etc.), I found myself leaving my hotel in Catete one sunny, very hot weekday afternoon, and, again, just walking.

Or maybe not just walking, because I was certainly thinking about a lot of things. (Things like what I had, in fact, learned here concerning Machado de Assis and his work, as well as, and more importantly, a new friendship I had formed with a Brazilian ex-diplomat/poet, whom I'd been told by a Brazilian acquaintance in Austin to contact in Rio.

The acquaintance had assured me that the ex-diplomat/poet would be somebody I could talk to about Brazilian literature and who also represented a long tradition of the country's writers often having careers in the foreign service. I had spent a wonderful afternoon with him—an older man and a bachelor himself—out at his sprawling and pretty cluttered apartment in an aging tropical high-rise in Copacabana, a thunderstorm pounding darkly outside as we talked for several hours about literature ranging well beyond that of only his native Brazil. Since that session, he had been phoning me at the hotel just about every morning, for long, intense conversations on many more matters literary. The talk could involve an assortment of topics, including his extended, and damn interesting, ruminating in his whispery voice about the comparative poetic potentials of various languages, of which he spoke several—French versus English versus Portuguese, let's say—and also what he had noticed just the night before in reading a collection of my short stories I had given him; that call came at nine in the morning on the day I took the walk, and, whispery-voiced as ever, he gently offered the observation that I had used the word "benevolent" twice within three pages in one short story and said that I should be careful of such slips, or I should always be as *very* careful as a poet even when writing fiction—and I knew he was right.) The small hotel I'd set myself up in was a fine and cheap enough family-run place in the Catete neighborhood, a few streets up from the sea and not far from the city center; the turn-of-the-century yellow building, formerly a townhouse, backed up to the public park that had once been the formal gardens of the very faded pink old presidential palace, when Catete—rundown and comfortably funky now—had actually been chic. There was no literary landmark of any variety I was looking for this day, though I did pass the inlet of Botafogo with its extensive sailboat harbor, a locale that turns up several times in Machado's work. I think I simply wanted to do what I hadn't yet done—go clear to the other side of Pão de Açúcar, the umber, rocket-shaped seaside mountain that is, of course, *the* Rio de Janeiro icon, and see the neighborhood of Urca; I had heard that it remained one of the most handsome older pockets of the city.

I could have gone out there by rattling city bus, but I decided that while it was a couple of miles, the route along the sea and beside the old winding expressway would be nice, perfect for walking. Not that walking in Rio was always entirely casual, I'd learned. One of the sad truths of this particular moment in Brazilian history was that street crime was rampant, a product of the larger truth that throughout Rio the Third World of utter poverty seems to be thrust flat against a First World of economic success and even outright glitz; the whole city is laced with steep, conical hills bearing mazes of makeshift tin-and-terracotta squatters' shacks, the *favela* slums that repeatedly rise up like maybe just so many remembered and very haunting dreams, everywhere. And I will admit I was a bit uneasy when I had to make my way through the urine-pungent pedestrian tunnel below the empty freeway and to the other side of it by the inlet at Botafogo, where there was a concrete concourse surrounding the tunnel's exit and a bus stop stranded there, no buildup of anything nearby. Men in rags—and some not men, only teenage boys—slept in nooks along the concrete walls splattered with graffiti; my being alone and obviously not Brazilian—somebody wandering uninvited through their sleep world, you might say—I undoubtedly stood out as a tourist, and one now in a territory where I really shouldn't be, at that. I usually kept a ready supply of coins for the shoeshine boys in Catete, to pay them *not* to shine my shoes and at least smilingly give them something, telling myself that I'd tried to help; here, however, it might not be that simple, I knew, and muggings, often at gunpoint, were rampant in Rio, almost to the stage of being mere commonplace occurrences and apparently part of the accepted give and take of daily city life. Nevertheless, once beyond the bleak concrete concourse at the tunnel, then taking a turn to the other side of Pão de Açúcar and walking down a wide, straight palm-lined boulevard in the heat—it must have been an even ninety degrees in December, Brazil's summer, with humidity to match—I felt a little stupid, or possibly guilty, for having been so apprehensive. While everybody I met in Rio kept warning me to always be careful and keenly on guard, I personally wanted to believe the situation *wasn't* as bad as often described.

I continued on, toward the village of Urca and the little beach I knew was there, called Praia Vermelha.

The boulevard stretched before me, with those tall, spindly palms and the roadway lanes divided by a grassy central island landscaped with overgrown oleander, the stars of the fleshy blossoms bursting white or pink. Steep and seemingly jungled emerald embankments rose up on both sides, and it was still empty on the sidewalk, though soon there were many more people for a while. Especially young people. They were obviously students, getting on and off the sooty yellow city buses with book packs, because in the stretch I now passed through was an older campus of the University of Rio de Janeiro; it continued to be used for some classes and lately was also a venue for conferences and the work of various research institutes. The fine nineteenth-century university buildings (formerly part of an asylum) faced the street and were sort of a wedding-cake architecture—Neoclassical and bright white—with lumpy red-tile roofs and no shortage of balustraded balconies and definitely "grand" front staircases, all surrounded by well-kept gardens and lawns. I could already see the sea up ahead, shimmering in the distance and at the end of the wide boulevard, where there seemed to be a rather formal, and somewhat out of place, open square.

And I could already smell the sea, along with the wafting perfumy fragrance that no matter where you are in Rio, a city of ever-blossoming flowers, does define the place. And here's where it gets tricky again, because continuing on toward the end of the boulevard, past some functional 1950s-style buildings now, squat high-rises painted pale green and part of the national military school, I started to anticipate something.

I mean, it was as if suddenly the whole outing wasn't merely a walk, and it was as if I was being drawn along, was moving toward something very definite even if I didn't know what it was, the soles of yet another pair of cushiony black-and-white nylon Reeboks rhythmically slapping, yes, I was moving with nearly somnambulistic conviction to whatever it was I would find at the end of this boulevard and the Praia Vermelha there at the sea waiting before me.

I passed what looked like a parade concourse for the military school, studded with a commemorative pillar, and there was a parking area, formed by a traffic-circle bulge in the boulevard, for the cable-car station that offered airy rides up to Pão de Açúcar; reportedly, the peak afforded spectacular views perhaps surpassed only by those from even higher up above Rio, at the enormous white statue of Christ the Redeemer with arms perpetually outstretched, perched on its own lofty mountain behind the city. And I then came to the end of the boulevard and the open square, empty. It was paved with large rectangular slabs of dark stone laid like tiles, and there were old-fashioned lampposts and benches, everything set at right angles and geometrically precise somehow, for a design that you couldn't quite peg as to period, or—this is it—pretty much timeless, I'd say, easily the stuff of a de Chirico painting. This square opened onto the perfect crescent of the little beach tucked in by the mountains, and the brown sands actually had a reddish tinge, living up to the name, Praia Vermelha. The low, glassy waves lapped lazily and whisperingly in the stillness of the day, and at the far edge of the square, on the side facing the water and at the exact midpoint of the plaza, was a single bronze statue—green going to black—set on a pedestal.

In the afternoon heat, I walked toward the figure.

Youthfully slim and hair swept back, dressed in breeches and high-collared jacket with a puffy cravat, Chopin was captured in a stance that had him romantically listing to one side, very contemplative and facing forever Guanabara Bay and the sea.

I stared at the statue. I'm not even sure whether what was provided on the plaque affixed to the granite pedestal sank in for me; there was some rubric explaining how the statue had been a gift of the Polish citizens of Brazil to their country, though in what year or to commemorate what particular occasion I would never really know or later investigate. But that didn't matter, and all that did matter while I stood there was that again, as on the walk in Paris, I had ended up where

I hadn't expected to have ended up. In other words, a rather random walk had taken me to a place—and a scene—I surely never expected to have come to, but it was, I fully knew now, a place where I very much wanted, and even needed, to be.

I looked out at the beach. It was no more than a few hundred feet wide and with but a dozen or so people in swimwear sitting here and there on low canvas chairs on this a weekday mid-afternoon. There were some fine waterfront villas, the handsomeness of the Urca architecture that I had read about in guidebooks, at the foot of the sheer stone cliffs on either side; farther out, where the water striped alternatingly aqua and a very dark blue, almost purple, was a long red-hulled freighter heading out to sea, moving toward the horizon, I guess, but in a way not moving whatsoever.

I sat down for a while on one of the benches in the open square. I slipped off my shoulder the little daypack I had been carrying and took out a bottle of mineral water, to slowly sip from it and think some more about things. (At this point in my life, unlike in Paris a few years earlier, there wasn't the woman in question to think about, and that hadn't worked out, though I wished it had. But there was more to think about concerning what the ex-diplomat/poet had told me, many things to think about on that front, also his latest poems that he had shown me as we sat together at the big mahogany dining room table in his apartment in Copa, his handing me the carefully typed sheets to read, some in English and some in French. They were good poems that I went through one by one as that thunderstorm outside intensified and as the younger man who lived with him—a pleasant, handsomely muscular Brazilian of African descent in T-shirt and shorts named José—did ironing in the kitchen then brought us a large pitcher of fresh-squeezed orange juice, smiling as he set it on the table, gentle and polite. I suppose that out at Praia Vermelha I even thought about the writer I had journeyed to Brazil to *think* about, Machado de Assis, the triumph of the novel *Epitaph of a Small Winner*, which had become, for a time, a veritable cause taken up by many contemporary American writers and that probably could rank as the single greatest contribution of all South American literature written in the nineteenth century, for me, anyway.) But to be honest, I have no recollection today exactly what I thought about while sitting on the bench.

There was just something about being there, something about the very concept of a lost little beach, more or less deserted, and a statue of Chopin contemplating forever the sea. And at this place, and as when I saw the travelers with the roller luggage all slowly moving toward the Gare Saint-Lazare, I realized it wasn't that this was a setting I was ever going to write about and use in a short story of my own.

It was just that overwhelming feeling, again and more than anything else in the world, that I wanted to be writing my fiction, getting back to it as soon as I could, in this case to somehow immediately dispose of the several thousand miles and many hours of an overnight jet hissing on and on through the darkness, then a change of planes in Atlanta and finally a taxi ride on the freeway back to my place in Austin. I wanted to write as much as I had ever wanted to in my entire life, including when I was a kid taking undergraduate creative writing classes to the point that I held some kind of record at my college then for the number of them taken, dreaming of someday publishing, or even when I did get some attention and good reviews on at least one of the books

I eventually went on to publish, granting the book never did sell very well—yet all of that had encouraged me, made me want to continue on with writing.

Or maybe this was so much more than anything I had known before. And right then and there I intensely wanted, now that I was indeed older and admittedly didn't have the luxury of any full arc of a career ahead of me, to once again be sitting down at my desk in the back room in my apartment there on a stubby cul-de-sac street in Austin, Texas, to simply be writing, even if so much else in my life—the failed relationships I didn't try hard enough to make work, a longtime job in a stifling English department in Austin where the so-called scholarly colleagues around me too often seemed like only busy careerists far removed from the genuinely important in literature, the students deserving better—true, just to be writing again seemed to be all that mattered, even if most everything else in my life, to be entirely honest about it, could at times feel as if it had never added up to very much.

I was still sitting on the bench.

"A statue of Chopin by the sea."

I think I whispered it aloud, liking the very sound of it; I sipped from the bottle again. The water was cool, and for insulation I had wrapped the clear plastic bottle in a thick towel from the hotel before leaving, an old trick I had learned years before in traveling.

I screwed the blue cap back onto the bottle, put the bottle back in the daypack, and zipped the thing up. I got up, slipped the pack's strap over one shoulder; I walked around the open square some more.

Two uniformed soldiers—young and smiling, from the nearby military school, most likely—were chatting with the guy who had a handcart marked PIPOCA at the far corner of the esplanade, under the limbs of a shading grove of eucalyptus trees; the cart on its bicycle wheels was a red contraption with shiny chrome trim, and the freshly popped corn itself, *pipoca*, lay heaped up high behind its glassed sides.

I listened a while longer to the low waves softly lapping on the sand before starting back toward the palm-lined boulevard, to finally wander through the sweet little neighborhood there directly below Pão de Açúcar, the whitewashed village of Urca proper and its maze of hilly side streets, everything impeccably groomed.

Until eventually, sure enough—and this is where it all gets stranger and even amazing, or that's the way I see it now, anyway—three days later I somehow *was* back at my desk in Austin again, putting together the words that as always (somehow magically? somehow inevitably a minor miracle?) became the sentences that became the paragraphs, as I worked on a new short story that was going well, one I was feeling very good about.

Which is to say—at the desk once more and at long last, I was *writing*.

2009, FROM *AGNI MAGAZINE*, AND ALSO
THE BEST AMERICAN TRAVEL WRITING 2010

PETER LaSALLE is the author of several books of fiction, most recently the novel *Mariposa's Song* and a short story collection, *What I Found Out About Her.* His work has appeared in many anthologies, including *The Best American Short Stories, The Best American Mystery Stories, Sports Best Stories,* and *Prize Stories: The O. Henry Awards.* Currently, he divides his time between Austin, Texas—where he is a member of the creative writing faculty at the University of Texas—and Narragansett in his native Rhode Island. He also continues to travel as much as possible to explore and write about the places where his favorite literature is set.